GAUGUIN DRAWINGS

John Rewald

GAUGUIN

DRAWINGS

A BITTNER ART BOOK

NEW YORK   THOMAS YOSELOFF   *LONDON*

© 1958 BY THOMAS YOSELOFF, INC.

LIBRARY OF CONGRESS CATALOGUE CARD NUMBER: 57-6896

THOMAS YOSELOFF, INC., NEW YORK

THOMAS YOSELOFF LTD., LONDON

PRINTED IN THE UNITED STATES OF AMERICA

BOOK DESIGN HERBERT BITTNER

FOR ALICE

IT MAY BE QUESTIONED WHETHER GAUGUIN WAS A "BORN" draftsman, but that he was a born painter there can be no doubt. Yet it took his innate gifts an unusually long time to come to the fore, and even then he was able to develop them only by dint of incredible persistence and through the process of a slow and not always too promising evolution. The sheer will to be an artist is, of course, not sufficient in itself to achieve mastery, for it does not replace natural qualifications, but the nineteenth century has witnessed several cases in which a complete devotion to art—often against considerable odds—was to yield astonishing results. Vincent van Gogh was such a case, and so was the *douanier* Rousseau; Gauguin was still another.

What makes Gauguin's case so fascinating is the fact that his strange and powerful personality seems literally to have stood in his way, and that his unending struggle, which led to such high accomplishments in art, was also a perpetual struggle against unfortunate dispositions which accentuated the difficulties of life rather than softened them.

Domineering by instinct, ferociously ambitious and at the same time childishly naïve, almost brazen in his self-confidence and yet subject to profound discouragements, shamelessly indulging in self-pity while proclaiming that the artist's calling set him outside the obligations and rules of modern society, entitling him to privileges while releasing him from the burden of responsibilities, always ready to justify his behavior as the artist's right to be different, willing to fight for the things in which he believed but also capable of compromises, quarrelsome, proud, demanding, ruthless, ungrateful, Gauguin lived a life of bitter trials. However, he never seems to have learned from experience, blindly trusting an intuition which again and again led him astray, always inclined to give in to illusions, to confound wishful thinking with reality, convinced of being endowed with a special sense for the practical. Calculating where it would have been better to trust, confident where he should have been suspicious, he threw himself into inextricable predicaments, and, the greater his misery, the more ardently he immersed himself in fantastic schemes. Such a disposition could only lead to innumerable conflicts and to his final, self-chosen isolation. But while he suffered beyond words and desperately fought for survival, while he was spared few humiliations and seldom knew the comfort of peaceful hours, there was one thing which sustained him and gave him the power to withstand the blows that fate dealt him: his conviction of his inner calling.

The inkling of this inner calling came comparatively late in Gauguin's life, after he had married and was well advanced in a career as a banker which seemed to assure success and wealth. He was twenty-five when he began to draw as a pastime, twenty-eight when he exhibited in 1875 a conventional landscape at the official Salon. At the same time he began to acquire a collection of paintings, and here he showed for the first time his independence of taste. For reasons which he never bothered to explain, he surrounded himself with works by Manet, Renoir, Monet, Pissarro, Sisley, Cézanne, etc., who were then still the laughingstock of the *cognoscenti* and must have looked singularly out of place in the home of a promising stockbroker. It was not much later that he met Camille Pissarro and thus embarked on a road that swiftly led him downhill socially while it rewarded him with the deep joys of creative work. Gauguin's first serious attempts at self-expression took place practically under the supervision of Pissarro. Although Pissarro never sought to instill his concepts into others, anxious rather to help them develop their own personalities, Gauguin's early works clearly show a great indebtedness to his first master.

Pissarro's advice to Gauguin must have been quite similar to that which he gave a few years later to his eldest son Lucien, whom he told to draw frequently and always from nature: "It is essential to have known forms in the eye and in the hand. It is only by drawing often, drawing everything, drawing incessantly, that one fine day you discover to your surprise that you have rendered something in its true character." And Pissarro also warned: "Do not be taken in by the facility of beginners; it is often an obstacle later on. So much the better if it is painful for you to take even the first step; the more toilsome the work the stronger you will emerge from it. Those who have more facility make less progress because they do well right away, with ease and without reflection; they are like the students with good memories. Of course, if one is strict with one's self, facility in execution can be an advantage. I repeat: guard against facility."

It does not appear as if Gauguin was blessed with that dangerous facility. His first sketchbooks reveal him as a rather uninspired draftsman, fairly timid and as yet unprepared to accentuate forms, to use shadows powerfully. His early models were his own children and other members of his household. A portrait of Pissarro which he drew in 1880 does not yet show any personality or particular promise. And a double portrait in which, on the same sheet, Pissarro drew a likeness of Gauguin and the latter a likeness of Pissarro, demonstrates graphically the sureness and incisiveness of the older man's pencil strokes as compared with Gauguin's

8

blurred lines and weak modeling. But soon he seems to have gained a firmer grasp on the possibilities of the black-and-white medium, and there are sketchbook pages which attest to his grappling with the oppositions of light and shadow, of line and form. His pastels, done apparently a little later, already show a great proficiency, although they, too, still lack originality in execution and color, coming as they did after the masterpieces which Manet was then creating with colored chalks.

In 1880 Gauguin for the first time exhibited some of his paintings with the Impressionist group to which he had been introduced by Pissarro. He now regularly spent his holidays in the country around Paris, working at Pissarro's side and occasionally also in company of the latter's friend Cézanne. Slowly his obsession with art became so strong that he was no longer satisfied merely to devote his spare time to it. In 1883, at the age of thirty-five, he quit his bank job so as to be a painter "every day," hoping to be able to earn a livelihood for himself and his large family—he now had five children—with an occupation from which he expected rapid fame and wealth. He left Paris and went to Rouen to join Pissarro, who wrote to his son: "Gauguin disturbs me very much; he is so deeply commercial, at least he gives that impression. I haven't the heart to point out to him how false and unpromising his attitude is. True, his needs are great, his family being used to luxury; just the same, his attitude can only hurt him. Not that I think we ought not try to sell, but I regard it a waste of time to think *only* of selling; one forgets one's art and exaggerates one's value." It did not take Gauguin very long to find this out by himself. Fate had no easy successes and rich rewards in store for him.

By now Gauguin had become a full-fledged—though minor—member of the Impressionist group. But since his new friends were still struggling for recognition, in spite of their much greater experience and more developed personalities, it cannot be surprising that Gauguin met with even greater difficulties. While his association with the Impressionists proved beneficial to the emergence of his artistic potentialities and taught him to use bright colors, he also derived a salutary lesson in draftsmanship from it. "To know how to draw does not mean to draw well," he later said. "Let us examine that famous science of draftsmanship—it is a science which all the pupils of the [official] Ecole des Beaux-Arts own, . . . a science that all, without exception, have acquired in a few years, like docile sheep led by their shepherd. . . . A painter who never knew how to draw but who draws well is Renoir. . . . Don't look for lines [in his work], they don't exist; through magic a lovely spot of color, a caressing light speak sufficiently for themselves."

Strangely enough, Renoir soon was to begin searching beyond those lovely spots of color, those modulations of light, and to revert to more linear concepts as a means to overreach Impressionism. As to Gauguin, while he admired Renoir's Impressionist style, he was not tempted by it, steeped as he was in Pissarro's more robust concern with solid forms. His evolution, too, was to lead toward an accentuation of line. But of this he was as yet scarcely conscious.

The years which followed Gauguin's fateful decision to abandon finance in favor of art were filled with tribulations and disappointments, yet they also stiffened his determination to be an artist. After a stay in Copenhagen where he half-heartedly tried to represent some commercial firms in a vain effort to appease his wife and her family, and after an attempt to exhibit his—still rather tame—works was thwarted by the Royal Danish Academy which ordered his show closed shortly after it had opened, Gauguin resolved to leave his family in Denmark and returned to Paris. He spent the rest of the year 1885 in Brittany, the winter in great misery in Paris, participated once more in the exhibition of the Impressionist group in 1886 (their last show), bitterly quarreled with Seurat whose theories he scorned, and eventually returned to Pont-Aven in Brittany where he made friends with a young painter, Charles Laval. In the fall he was back in Paris, worked on ceramics with Chaplet, and met Vincent van Gogh. In April, 1887, Gauguin, accompanied by Laval, sailed for Panama and thence for Martinique, driven by a constant longing for tropical colors and subjects.

Gauguin's sojourn in Martinique soon turned into another calamity, despite his initial enthusiasm for the luxuriant vegetation and the elegant bearing of the natives. Poorly adapted to the climate, the two friends fell seriously ill and Laval even attempted to commit suicide. After a few months they had but one thought: return to France, a return which had to be postponed for lack of funds. But before the year was over, they were back in Paris.

In one of his rare letters from Martinique, Gauguin wrote: "What tempts me most are the figures. Every day there is a continuous coming and going of Negresses attired in colorful rags, their graceful movements infinitely varied. For the time being I am merely making sketch after sketch in order to grasp their character, but later I shall ask them to pose." However, only very few of these sketches seem to exist, possibly because the artist left them behind when—ill and discouraged —he returned to Europe. Those that have been preserved show no radical departure from his previous style, for it was not in his draftsmanship but in his color schemes that Gauguin's contact with the tropics brought about the greatest change. His palette brightened, contrasts became more accentuated, the pale softness of earlier works slowly disappeared. At the same time his composition began to reveal a slight Japanese influence, and sometimes there appeared in his canvases large areas of comparatively uniform color. Yet his paintings, when he exhibited them in Paris, disappointed his few admirers who had expected more sweeping conquests of color and an open break with Impressionism; they found neither in his scenes from Martinique.

It was only after his arrival from the West Indian island that Gauguin was to search for a radically new departure, for a more personal expression. He returned once more to Pont-Aven in Brittany. During the summer of 1888, in the company of an ardent youngster, Emile Bernard, Gauguin started a remarkable evolution. Bernard, only twenty years old, had already fathered a new style, Cloisonism, which divided a painting into differently colored compartments, analogous to the medieval *cloisonné* technique. This procedure demanded that the painter "trace his drawing in closed lines between which he puts varied hues, the juxtaposition of which will provide the sensation of the general coloration intended, the drawing emphasizing the color and color emphasizing the design."

This new concept not only offered means to overcome Impressionism, of which Gauguin had grown weary, but it also put a strong accent on linear arrangements with which Gauguin had barely begun to concern himself. Whatever the extent of Bernard's share in Gauguin's artistic development may have been, Bernard's ideas and Gauguin's daily contact with him translated themselves in a feverish activity and in a succession of works in which Gauguin's "Synthetism" began to emerge. Their productive community of work, their constant exchange of ideas, led them on a road to new discoveries and achievements, toward a style which neither could claim as solely his own and which—when other less gifted men followed their lead—became known as the style of the Pont-Aven "school."

Henceforth Gauguin was to be preoccupied with what he called "the *synthesis* of form and color derived from the observation of the dominant element only." To a painter-friend he now offered this advice: "Don't copy nature too much. Art is an abstraction; derive this abstraction from nature while dreaming before it." The goal was to reduce all forms to their essential outlines, to use pure colors, to avoid shadows so far as possible, and even to renounce modeling to a great extent. Such concepts evidently demanded a different kind of drawing from the one Gauguin had practiced until then. Careful shadings and subtle degradations had to be abandoned in favor of strong contours.

During that summer of 1888, Gauguin spent a great deal of time making drawings, though some of his sketchbooks of the period seem richer in "doodles" than in finished products. But even in the slightest notations he shows himself preoccupied with simplification of forms and strong contrasts of black and white. In his paintings, of course, he could and did heighten the effect of sinuous lines by oppositions of color and thus achieved a particularly powerful stylization.

Yet it was not in Brittany that Gaugin executed the drawing most representative of his new manner. That drawing was made in Arles, during those fateful last months of the year 1888 which Gauguin spent with Vincent van Gogh in Provence. Whether he wanted to show his friend to what degree he could simplify lines, flatten planes, synthetize forms, or whether the picturesque black-and-white costumes of Arlesian women lent themselves particularly to a representation based on simple contrasts of light and dark, the fact remains that Gauguin's drawing of an *Arlésienne* expresses all the startling features of his recent evolution. Similar preoccupations appear also in the few watercolors Gauguin made in Arles, strong color accents—bright reds and greens, strong yellows and blacks—enhancing the broadly conceived and powerfully outlined forms.

After the dramatic incident during which van Gogh temporarily lost his mind, and after Gauguin's hasty return to Paris, he composed, in the company of Bernard, a series of lithographs—drawn on zinc instead of stone—which may be called his first "independent drawings," meant to be considered by themselves, as autonomous works of art, whereas most of his previous drawings had been either studies for paintings or exercises to master the graphic medium. Basically, lithographs are nothing but drawings, executed with a special ink on plates or stones from which they can be pulled in a limited number of copies. Gauguin's first lithographs are, with few exceptions, repetitions of subjects he had previously treated in paintings; one might almost say that he drew reproductions of his canvases. He varied the effects by choosing as models works painted in Brittany as well as in Martinique and in Arles. Throughout his life he was to follow a similar procedure, later executing woodcuts of Tahitian subjects in Brittany or painting recollections of Breton scenes in the South Seas.

Gauguin thought enough of his lithographs to exhibit them in the memorable show organized in the Café Volpini during the Paris World's Fair of 1889, where he and Bernard gathered around them some of their followers of Pont-Aven and where the new "Synthetist" style for the first time manifested itself in public. It met with little attention, and Gauguin's lithographs, in particular, seem to have

12

aroused scant interest. It is true that their flat planes, their deep blacks, their sometimes clumsy execution, and their unorthodox compositions—again vaguely reminiscent of the Japanese—were features hardly designed to be accepted at a time when the Impressionists themselves were still not deemed worthy to be represented at the World's Fair.

PASTORALE MARTINIQUE   A   1889

Back in Brittany, deeply discouraged by the failure of the exhibition on which he had pinned great hopes, Gauguin resumed his painting and also did some watercolors; but he does not seem to have drawn very much. Instead, he made sculptures, bas-reliefs, painted murals, decorated furniture, did designs for plates, and explored so many different avenues that some of his friends actually thought that "he was going to change his style." Yet he was merely hiding his despondency behind frantic research in various directions, behind a sometimes febrile activity, whereas

13

at other moments he was so dispirited that he abandoned work altogether. "Almost mechanically," he wrote to Bernard, "I make some studies (if one can call studies a few brush strokes determined by the eye). But the soul is not there; sadly it observes the gaping hole in front of it."

It was in this frame of mind that Gauguin began to dream once more of tropical climes, of a primitive life, of exotic subjects. Forgotten the sad experiences of Martinique, illness, and poverty. Whenever his spirits were particularly low, he seems to have found solace in enticing images of South Sea paradises where life was carefree, people were friendly, women attractive, and pictorial subjects plentiful. After various efforts to find a sponsor for a new trip had come to naught, Gauguin resolved, late in 1890, to return to Paris in order to raise the necessary funds by any available means.

During that winter of 1890–91, the artist fell in with a group of Parisian writers and poets who, only a few years before, had launched the still controversial movement of literary Symbolism and who now hailed Gauguin as their counterpart in the visual arts. After his long isolation in Brittany, where the company of a few admirers—such as the painter Meyer de Haan—had not provided sufficient stimulus, Gauguin was delighted to find himself acclaimed a "Symbolist" painter. He assiduously attended the gatherings of his new friends in various cafés. There he met among others the leaders of the movement, Mallarmé and Moréas, of whom he was to draw portraits; his likeness of Moréas is particularly fraught with symbolic elements. In the company of these men Gauguin discussed at great length the merits of other painters admired by the poets, such as Puvis de Chavannes, whose influence appears in some of Gauguin's Tahitian compositions, Carrière, whom he befriended and even feebly imitated for a short while, but above all Redon, whom he saw frequently and whose mysterious art left a deep impression on him (a number of his subsequent works show vague souvenirs of Redon's style, his colors, his particular brand of imagination). At the same time Gauguin endeavored to sum up the main elements of his own style in a large canvas, *The Loss of Virginity*, for which he did a drawing that, in its powerful contrasts and sinuous lines, resumes the achievements of his *Arlésienne*.

After an auction sale in February, 1891, where his works commanded adequate prices, and after a banquet in his honor where the Symbolist poets toasted him, Gauguin left for Tahiti early in April.

Gauguin himself has set forth, in his book *Noa Noa*, what his first impressions of Tahiti were; how he was soon disappointed with Papeete and decided to live close to nature; how he settled in the wilderness, observing the natives, slowly learning their language; how he studied their fascinating lore, penetrating himself with their superstitions and beliefs; but above all how he found an ideal companion in lovely young Tehura—how he tried to forget Europe and to become a "savage."

Gauguin remembered later: "I began to work; notes and sketches of all kinds. But the landscape, with its bright, burning colors dazzled and blinded me. . . . And yet it was so simple to paint things as I saw them, to put on my canvas a red and a blue. . . . Why did I hesitate to let all that gold and all the joy of the sun flow directly onto my canvas?—Old routines of Europe, timidity of expression of degenerate races!" As he had done at Martinique, Gauguin apparently started to draw a great deal before he touched his brushes. In one of his first letters from Tahiti he reported: "I have put myself to work with determination. I can't say whether it's worth anything, for it is a good deal and it is nothing. Not yet a painting but a host of researches which may prove fruitful; a great many documents which will serve me for a long time, I hope—for example in France."

It seems that many of Gauguin's sketches, which he made either in small notebooks or on pieces of paper (later by him assembled in a portfolio: *Documents— Tahiti, 1891, 1892, 1893*), were executed during the first months, while his impressions were still new and before he dared use color. These studies constitute indeed a "documentation" of a peculiar kind. They show helter-skelter landscapes with lush vegetation, natives in various characteristic attitudes, squatting women, mothers nursing their babies, numerous heads of children, images of idols, tracings of ornamental designs, animals of all kinds, studies of plants and trees, nudes, details of hands and feet, etc. Some are lightly done, jotted down with a few pencil strokes, others are worked out carefully, a few have been redrawn with ink, to give their lines greater firmness, still others have been touched up with watercolor. But whether they are mere shorthand notes or products of careful study, none of them shows any preoccupation with a "finished" drawing to be shown or exhibited as a work of observation and skill. They all have the personal character of chance notations, filed away on small pieces of paper for possible later use. For this seems exactly to have been their purpose, what Gauguin meant when he wrote that he hoped his researches "may prove fruitful" and that he was accumulating "a great many documents which will serve me for a long time."

The "repertory" of figures, attitudes, gestures, details, etc., which Gauguin thus assembled during his first stay in Tahiti, was indeed to serve him for many years. He referred to it frequently in years to come, to the extent where it often becomes difficult to date his paintings; none of Gauguin's canvases can be dated simply because a drawing with similar features is known to have been executed at a specific time or place. Drawing and painting may be separated by a long period of time, and in some cases the drawing may even have been made *after* the completion of the picture. As a matter of fact, Gauguin liked to repeat in different compositions details of his works with which he was particularly pleased.

It is a strange fact that the man whose adventurous blood had led him to circle half of the globe in search of new inspiration, whose adventurous mind had prompted him to seek out new stylistic expressions, should have been much less adventurous in his actual methods of work. Once he had constituted his "repertory" of Tahitian observations, occasionally developed into more elaborate and larger drawings, he used it with little changes throughout his work. Since he was not primarily a draftsman and possibly had only through great efforts achieved some gratifying results, he must have considered it "safer" to incorporate into his compositions elements he found satisfying (having utilized them successfully before) rather than search for something new and different. It is not in his landscapes, though, but in his figures that these constant repetitions occur. He was apt to exploit a sketch of a figure in a painting, in a sculpture or wood relief, in a watercolor, a monotype, a woodcut, and later to use it as part of a composition. Thus Tahitian women, in a number of favored attitudes, people the works of his last ten to twelve years, appearing here in the foreground, there in the background of a canvas, sometimes repeated without changes, sometimes their posture slightly varied, sometimes their heads interchanged or their bodies reversed, facing left instead of right. (It was easy to obtain such "reversals." The artist merely drew his original sketch with the paper lying on some soft, possibly moist ochre ground, which left a tracing on the back of his sheet. By turning the paper, Gauguin had a perfect reversed copy of his initial study. Subsequently, when he made woodcuts, his compositions were of course automatically reversed in the printed proof.)

Gauguin was "un-adventurous" in still another way: he usually preferred straight front-views, profiles, or back-views for his figures; three-quarter angles and *profils perdus* are comparatively rare in his work. The few three-quarter views of heads which he deemed satisfactory are repeated possibly more often than any of the other elements of his artistic repertory. Having thus to a certain extent simplified his task, Gauguin was able to concentrate more fully on problems of color. Toward the end of his life he was to say: "I never knew how to make a

16

real drawing, how to manipulate an eraser, etc. It always seemed to me that something was missing: *the color*." But this was an understatement, for Gauguin did make in Tahiti a great many important drawings in black and white, though he also frequently worked with colored chalks and water color. However, comparatively few even of his large drawings are signed, that is, bear the stamp of his satisfaction.

When he returned to France in the summer of 1893, once more penniless, ill, disheartened, and deeply disillusioned, Gauguin brought back not only numerous small sketches but also a series of large drawings of unequaled splendor: Tahitian natives in picturesque attitudes, nudes of powerful and simple lines, watercolors with vivid accents conveying the glory of blazing vistas, monotypes with subtle shadings, and compositions with mysterious idols and dreamlike scenes, akin to Redon's imaginary world (not to speak of his most important "booty," a group of canvases in which he had captured the indescribable radiance of the tropics). He also brought back a strange notebook, its pages filled with passages copied from an ancient book on island lore. These pages were illustrated with odd and barbaric images, almost crudely colored, among them scenes from the natives' love life. This notebook was to form the basis for his manuscript, *Noa Noa,* written in France with the assistance of the Symbolist poet Charles Morice and telling the moving story of Gauguin's experiences in Tahiti. The manuscript of *Noa Noa* he illustrated even more profusely, not only with watercolors and drawings, but also with photographs and woodcuts pasted onto its pages (some of them colored by the artist), a true "scrapbook" of Gauguin's Tahitian adventure. It was first published without any of the illustrations, accompanied instead by poems Morice wrote around the painter's text.

During that stay in France, part of which Gauguin spent again in Brittany, he also made a series of woodcuts, all of Tahitian subjects, for which he used the many sketches he had accumulated in the South Seas. These woodcuts were for him an altogether new departure, for he tried to achieve with this new medium an expression he could not obtain with any other. Though they were based on his drawings, Gauguin's woodcuts are conceived in terms of the wood itself; not merely linear arrangements transposed on a wood block, they derive their specific character from the wood and the tools with which he executed them. Behind their sometimes willfully rough execution Gauguin hid the most precious refinements of conception and style. While his woodcuts in no way resemble his drawings, they share with them the distinguishing features of his art: a tremendous gift for simplification, a delight in playing with forms—opposing dark masses to delicately treated areas—a European sensitiveness combined with "barbaric" subjects.

AUTI TE PAPE (WOMEN AT A RIVER) ᴮ   1894

It is difficult to say whether Gauguin made many drawings during this sojourn in France which extended from 1893 to 1895, preoccupied as he was with exploring the possibilities of the woodcut, with writing his memoirs and illustrating them. Even in his painted work those years do not represent any specific phase of new or startling achievements. Eventually Europe could hold him no longer. The spell cast by Tahiti would not release him from its grip, bitter though some of his experiences had been there. After he had run through a small inheritance, had been wounded in a fight with drunken sailors, had been laid up for weeks, had been abandoned by his latest mistress, but—above all—had failed to sell any paintings at an exhibition which assembled his most important Tahitian canvases, he resolved to organize another auction and to leave once more, this time forever. In July, 1895, he arrived again in Papeete.

Gauguin's last years in Tahiti and later in Atuana on one of the Marquesas Islands were a heartbreaking succession of illness, debts, and despondency, every now and then interrupted by phases of active work. Early in 1898 the pressure of

18

isolation and worries became too much. He decided to kill himself, but first wished to paint a last, large canvas, *Whence Do We Come? What Are We? Where Are We Going?*—a kind of artistic testament, vaguely related in concept to Puvis de Chavannes' murals. His suicide attempt having failed, he had no choice but to resume his life of suffering and creative efforts. He became increasingly quarrelsome and soon found himself at odds with the French colonial administrators, having taken it upon himself to defend the natives against the often objectionable measures of the French officials. This attitude did not exactly endear him to his countrymen, and their resentment further added to his difficulties, until he found himself eventually convicted for defamation.

LOST PARADISE   C   1895–1903

The drawings which Gauguin made during those last years do not distinguish themselves basically from those of his previous trip. Were it not that some are closely related to paintings which bear a date, it would be difficult to establish even a vague chronology. He seems to have drawn less than before, possibly because he now devoted considerable time to woodcuts (these woodcuts are done on coarser wood and with cruder tools than those executed in Brittany and therefore have a more primitive aspect.)

During the last months of his life, Gauguin illustrated another important manuscript, *Avant et Après,* a strange hodgepodge of recollections, bilious comments, anecdotes, press clippings, and considerations on art. Unlike the illustrations for *Noa Noa,* these are all in black and white, either drawn with pen and ink or executed in monotype. They abound in hatchings and small strokes and only seldom show the startling contrasts of light and dark masses, for which he had now found a better suited medium in the woodcut.

When Gauguin died on May 8, 1903, in Atuana—before he could appeal his conviction—few canvases were left in his hut, for these he had periodically shipped to Vollard in Paris, who had become his dealer and irregularly sent him meager remittances. But there were many drawings, besides wood carvings, etc. Of these the gendarmes diligently destroyed all those they considered "obscene," others were left to rot, some were sold in bundles at an auction in Papeete. Most of them are lost forever. Thus have disappeared not only artistic treasures, but also a valuable record of Gauguin's most intimate work. Indeed, he considered his drawings personal memos which were not destined for the public. He did not even wish to show them, anxious without doubt to turn to them, as he had done before, as a repertory of forms and observations to be used in his canvases. Had he not, shortly before his death, written in *Avant et Après:*

"A critic comes to see my paintings and, somewhat hesitantly, asks for my drawings. My drawings! Oh, no! They are my private letters, my secrets."

JOHN REWALD

ILLUSTRATIONS IN THE TEXT

PASTORALE MARTINIQUE, 1889
Lithograph, 8⅜″ x 10⅜″. Executed in Paris. The Museum of Modern Art, New York
(Lillie P. Bliss Collection).

AUTI TE PAPE (WOMEN AT A RIVER), 1894
Woodcut, 8⅛″ x 14″. Executed in Brittany. The Museum of Modern Art, New York
(Lillie P. Bliss Collection).

LOST PARADISE, 1895–1903
Woodcut. Executed in Tahiti or Atuana. The City Art Museum of St. Louis (Gift of
Vincent Price).

Except for minor concessions to the harmony of the layout, the reproductions have been arranged chronologically so far as that is possible.

It should be stressed, however, that many of the dates here assigned to individual works are based on deductions and stylistic considerations rather than on known facts, since Gauguin's drawings are practically never dated. It is partly for this reason that the comments in the list of plates give ample references to paintings, prints, etc., in which similar elements appear.

LIST OF PLATES

FRANCE (1880–91)

1 HEAD OF A WOMAN, c. 1884

Pastel, 11½″ x 9″. Page from a sketch-book. Collection Mr. and Mrs. Herbert Mayer, New York. Photo John D. Schiff, New York.

2 STUDIES OF A WOMAN'S HEAD, 1884–85

Charcoal, 9″ x 11½″. Page from a sketch-book. Collection Mr. and Mrs. Herbert Mayer, New York. Photo John D. Schiff, New York.

3 PORTRAIT OF THE ARTIST'S SON, CLOVIS, c. 1885

Pastel, 10¾″ x 10″. Present whereabouts unknown. Photo Knoedler & Co., New York.

4 PORTRAIT OF PAUL GAUGUIN BY PISSARRO—PORTRAIT OF CA-MILLE PISSARRO BY GAUGUIN, c. 1883

Pencil, Musée du Louvre, Paris.

This double portrait was doubtlessly drawn during one of the vacation periods which the then bank employee Gauguin used to spend with Pissarro at

Pontoise or Osny; it formerly belonged to Pissarro.

5 PORTRAIT OF CAMILLE PISSARRO, 1880

Pencil, 8⅞″ x 7⅞″. Collection Fru Urban Gad, Copenhagen. Photo courtesy Dr. Haavard Rostrup, Copenhagen.

One of the earliest known drawings by Gauguin; it was formerly in the possession of the artist's wife, *née* Gad.

6 SEATED BRITTANY WOMAN, 1886(?)

Charcoal and pastel, 12⅞″ x 19″. The Art Institute of Chicago (Gift of Carter H. Harrison).

This study is dedicated to Charles Laval. The fact that Gauguin used the formal designation "M. Laval" in his inscription makes it appear likely that it was given to his friend before the two men went together to Martinique.

7 TWO WOMEN FROM MARTI-NIQUE, 1887

Charcoal and pastel. Present whereabouts unknown. Photo Vizzavona, Paris.

The same two figures appear in a painting from Martinique, *Fruit Pickers*, in the collection of Ir. V. W. van Gogh, Laren, Holland, reproduced in J. Rewald: *Post-Impressionism—from van Gogh to Gauguin*, New York, 1956, p. 75.

8 HEAD OF A BRETON WOMAN, 1888–90

Charcoal, 11½″ x 12¼″. The Art Institute of Chicago. Photo H. Benezit, Paris.

9 HEAD OF A BRETON BOY, c. 1888

Pastel, 7¾″ x 7½″. Collection Mr. and Mrs. George N. Richard, New York. Photo Wildenstein & Co., New York.

This is apparently the same boy represented on plate 12.

10 BRETON WOMAN SEEN FROM THE BACK, c. 1888

Pastel, 18″ x 11⅞″. Present whereabouts unknown. Photo Dixon & Son, London.

Study for the central figure of a painting of Breton peasant women in the Bayerische Staatsgemäldesammlungen, Munich (reproduced in the catalogue of the Gauguin exhibition, Kunstmuseum, Basel, November, 1949–January, 1950, No. 17). Although this canvas is dated 1886, it is generally agreed that it must have been painted in 1888. See also the lithograph catalogued in M. Guérin: *L'Oeuvre gravé de Gauguin*, Paris, 1927, No. 4.

11 YOUNG BRETON GIRL KNITTING, 1889

Pastel. Present whereabouts unknown. Photo Vizzavona, Paris.

Study for the painting *Girl Tending Pigs, Brittany*, dated 1889 (reproduced in Rewald: *Gauguin*, Paris and New York, 1938, p. 86), formerly in the collection of G. Daniel de Monfreid.

12 YOUNG BRETON BATHER, 1888

Pastel. Present whereabouts unknown. Photo Vizzavona, Paris.

Study for a painting, dated 1888, formerly in the collection of W. Weinberg, Scarsdale, New York, reproduced in Rewald: *Gauguin*, p. 71.

13 WOMAN BATHER IN BRITTANY, 1887(?)

Charcoal and pastel, 22½″ x 13⅝″. The Art Institute of Chicago (Gift of Mr. and Mrs. Charles B. Goodspeed).

Study for the painting, dated 1887, reproduced in Rewald: *Gauguin*, p. 70. The catalogue of the Gauguin exhibition, Kunstmuseum, Basel, November, 1949–January 1950, lists under No. 108 a sketch for a fan, representing the same subject and dated 1887, which is supposed to have been made at Martinique. But this does not seem very likely, since the painting in which this bather appears clearly shows a Breton landscape. It is possible that the present drawing was made in Brittany in 1886 and used for both the painting and the fan early in 1887, before Gauguin left for Martinique. See also Guérin, *op. cit.*, No. 3.

14 HEAD OF A BRETON GIRL, c. 1889(?)

Pencil, crayon, and wash, 8¾″ x 7⅞″. Fogg Art Museum, Harvard University, Cambridge, Massachusetts (Meta and Paul J. Sachs Collection).

15 L'ARLÉSIENNE, 1888

Charcoal, 28″ x 19″. Collection T. E. Hanley, Bradford, Pennsylvania. Photo S. Sunami, New York.

This drawing was made during Gauguin's short stay with Vincent van Gogh at Arles as a study for a painting, *The Night Café*, in the Museum of Modern Western Art, Moscow (reproduced in Rewald: *Post-Impressionism*, p. 251). Vincent van Gogh, who owned this drawing, painted several versions of *L'Arlésienne* from it, while in Saint-Rémy.

16 WASHERWOMEN AT ARLES, 1888

Watercolor on silk. Collection Arthur Sachs, Paris.

There exists a painting of the same subject, reproduced in Rewald: *Post-Impressionism*, p. 258.

17 WASHERWOMEN AT ARLES, 1888

Watercolor on silk. Present whereabouts unknown. Photo Vizzavona, Paris.

See also the lithograph of the same subject (Guérin, *op. cit.*, No. 6).

18 PEASANT GIRL AT LE POULDU (*Brittany*), 1889

Watercolor on silk, 7¼″ x 4⅛″. Private collection, New York. Photo Wildenstein & Co., New York.

The same figure appears in the painting *Bonjour Monsieur Gauguin*, dated 1889, in the Museum of Prague (reproduced in Rewald: *Gauguin*, p. 86).

19 STUDY FOR "THE YELLOW CHRIST," 1889

Pencil, 12½″ x 9½″. Collection Mr. and Mrs. William Goetz, Los Angeles, California.

The painting, one of the most important examples of Gauguin's "Synthetist" style, is in the Albright Art Gallery, Buffalo, New York (reproduced in Rewald: *Gauguin*, p. 80). See also plate 20.

20 THE YELLOW CHRIST, 1889

Watercolor, 6″ x 5″. Collection Mrs. Gilbert W. Chapman, New York.

See also plate 19 and the notice for that plate.

21 MISÈRES HUMAINES (*Brittany*), c. 1888

Watercolor. Present whereabouts unknown. Photo Vizzavona, Paris.

See also the lithograph (Guérin, *op. cit.*, No. 5). The figure of the young girl appears also in a painting of the same title in the Art Institute of Chicago (reproduced in Rewald: *Post-Impressionism*, p. 286), as well as in the painting *Vineyard at Arles with Breton Women*, dated 1888, in the Ordrupgaardsamlingen, Copenhagen (reproduced *ibid.*, p. 253). Gauguin represented the same figure once more in a woodcut done in Tahiti (see Guérin, *op. cit.*, No. 69).

22 EVE, c. 1889

Pastel and watercolor, 13¼″ x 12½″. Marion Koogler McNay Art Institute, San Antonio, Texas. Photo Vizzavona, Paris.

This may well be the work which Gauguin exhibited at the "Exposition impressionniste et synthétiste," in the Café Volpini, Paris, during the 1889 World's Fair, under the title *Pas écouter li li menteur* (a childish spelling of "Don't listen to the liar"). The same figure appears also in the background of plate 25.

23 STUDIES FOR POTTERY, 1887–89

Charcoal and watercolor, 12½" x 16⅜". Knoedler & Co., New York.

Around 1888, Gauguin worked on various potteries with the ceramist Chaplet. A vase corresponding to the left and center studies on this sheet is reproduced opposite p. 4 of the catalogue of the exhibition "Gauguin, sculpteur et graveur," Luxembourg Museum, Paris, January–February, 1928.

24 LES FOLIES DE L'[AMOUR], 1890

Watercolor and gouache, 12½" in diameter. Private collection, New York. Photo Justin K. Thannhauser, New York.

Design for a plate, executed in Brittany. For other designs see Rewald: *Post-Impressionism*, p. 300; also Guérin, *op. cit.*, No. 1. This plate is dated in jest 1290.

25 NIRVANA—PORTRAIT OF JACOB MEYER DE HAAN (*Brittany*), c. 1890

Gouache on silk, 8" x 11⅛". Wadsworth Atheneum, Hartford, Connecticut. Photo Wildenstein & Co., New York.

For one of the figures in the background, see plate 22; the other figure appears in a painting, *Woman in Waves*, in the collection of Mr. and Mrs. W. Powell Jones, Cleveland, Ohio (reproduced in the catalogue of the Gauguin exhibition, Wildenstein Galleries, New York, April–May, 1956, p. 37, No. 18).

26 STUDY FOR A PORTRAIT OF JACOB MEYER DE HAAN (*Brittany*), c. 1890

Water color, 5½" x 7⅜". Wildenstein & Co., New York.

The slight sketch of a figure at the right appears related to plate 14. Gauguin was fascinated with his friend's startling features and later represented them in various Tahitian paintings.

27 YOUNG GIRL AND FOX—STUDY FOR "LOSS OF VIRGINITY" (*Paris*), 1890–91

Charcoal on yellow paper, 13" x 13". Collection Mr. and Mrs. Leigh B. Block, Chicago, Illinois. Photo Wildenstein & Co., New York.

Juliette Huet, who posed for this drawing, was Gauguin's mistress in Paris during the winter 1890–91. The painting *Loss of Virginity*, in the collection of Walter P. Chrysler, Jr., New York (reproduced in Rewald: *Post-Impressionism*, p. 466), was an attempt by the artist to express in a large canvas his "Symbolist" ideas which had been kindled by his recent acquaintance with the leaders of literary Symbolism. On this painting, see D. Sutton: "*La Perte du Pucelage* by Paul Gauguin," *Burlington Magazine*, April, 1949.

28 PORTRAIT OF STÉPHANE MALLARMÉ, 1891

Pencil and pen and ink, 10" x 7½". Formerly collection A. Vollard, Paris; present whereabouts unknown.

This is a study for an etching (see Guérin, *op. cit.*, Nos. 13–14) which also features the raven—sketched in the upper right—inspired by Mallarmé's translation of Edgar Allan Poe's poem.

29 HEAD OF A CHILD, c. 1890

Charcoal. Collection Georges Renand, Paris.

Gauguin painted two likenesses of this child (see M. Malingue: *Gauguin*, Paris, 1948, pp. 134 and 135). This drawing was part of a portfolio of studies which the artist had labeled *Documents Tahiti—1891, 1892, 1893*, but which apparently also contained some sketches dating from his Breton period, as is the case for this drawing. On this portfolio see the catalogue of the "Exposition Gauguin—Aquarelles, Monotypes, Dessins," Galerie Marcel Guiot, Paris, May 15–June 13, 1942.

30 SOYEZ SYMBOLISTE—PORTRAIT OF JEAN MORÉAS, 1890–91

Brush and pen and ink. Collection Georges Renand, Paris.

Together with plates 27 and 28, this is one of the rare mementos of Gauguin's "Symbolist" endeavors inspired by his association with the Symbolist poets in Paris.

TAHITI (1891–93)

31 HEAD OF A TAHITIAN CHILD, c. 1891

Pencil and watercolor. Page from a sketchbook(?). Present whereabouts unknown.

32 HEAD OF A YOUNG TAHITIAN BOY, TETUA, c. 1891

Pencil and ink, 6½″ x 4¼″. Collection Mr. and Mrs. Alex M. Lewyt, New York. Photo John D. Schiff, New York.

33 HEAD OF A YOUNG TAHITIAN BOY, FARE, c. 1891

Pencil and ink, 6½″ x 4¼″. Collection Mr. and Mrs. Alex M. Lewyt, New York. Photo John D. Schiff, New York.

34 HEAD OF A YOUNG TAHITIAN BOY, TASA, c. 1891

Pencil and ink, 6½″ x 4¼″. Collection Mr. and Mrs. Alex M. Lewyt, New York. Photo John D. Schiff, New York.

Plates 32–34 may be studies for the painting *The Repast*, dated 1891, given to the Musée du Louvre, Paris, by André Meyer (reproduced in Rewald: *Post-Impressionism*, p. 499). These three drawings (also plate 45) were originally part of a small sketchbook from Gauguin's first trip to Tahiti (see Paul Gauguin: *Carnet de Tahiti*, facsimile edition with an introduction by B. Dorival, Paris, 1954).

35 SKETCHES (*Tahiti*), 1891–93

Pencil, pen and ink, and watercolor. Present whereabouts unknown. Photo Vizzavona, Paris.

36 SKETCHES (*Tahiti*), 1891–93

Charcoal and watercolor, 9½″ x 12¼″ Musée du Louvre, Paris. Photo Routhier, Paris (courtesy Paul Brame & César de Hauke).

37 TAHITIAN GIRL STRETCHED OUT, c. 1893

Charcoal. Present whereabouts unknown. Photo Marcel Guiot, Paris.

Study for the painting *Siesta* (*On the Terrace*), 1893, in the collection of Mr. and Mrs. Ira Haupt, New York (reproduced in Rewald: *Post-Impressionism*, p. 533). The drawings reproduced on plates 37–41 were part of the portfolio described in the notice for plate 29.

38 TAHITIAN WOMAN SQUATTING, 1891–93(?)

Monotype. Present whereabouts unknown. Photo Marcel Guiot, Paris.

The same figure appears in the painting *Why Are You Angry?* (*No te aha oe riri*), dated 1896, in the Art Institute of Chicago (reproduced in Rewald: *Gauguin*, p. 115), as well as in the painting *The Sister of Charity*, dated 1902, in the Marion Koogler McNay Art Institute, San Antonio, Texas (reproduced in Malingue, *op. cit.*, p. 228). A similar drawing is also to be found on p. 179 of Gauguin's manuscript of *Avant et Après*. Since all these works date from the artist's second sojourn in the South Seas, this monotype might have been executed between 1895 and 1903, were it not for the fact that it was part of the portfolio described in the notice for plate 29 and that the sketchbook from the first trip to Tahiti, described in the notice for plate 34, features opposite p. 98 another study for the painting *The Sister of Charity*. A similar drawing belongs to the Musée du Louvre, and a third one is reproduced on p. 24 of the catalogue described in the notice for plate 29. All of these belonged to the 1891–93 portfolio.

39 CROUCHING TAHITIAN GIRL, 1891–93

Pencil, 7⅛" x 5⅛". Collection M. Français, Paris. Photo Marcel Guiot, Paris.

Study for the painting *The Idol*, reproduced on p. 140 of Rewald: *Gauguin*. The same figure in reverse appears in the painting *Et l'or de leurs corps*, dated 1901, in the Musée du Louvre (reproduced *ibid.*, p. 145), as well as in the woodcut, Guérin, *op. cit.*, No. 35. See also plate 63 and the notice for that plate.

40 STUDY FOR "WORDS OF THE DEVIL" (PARAU NA TE VARUA INO), 1891–92

Pencil, 8⅞" x 8½". Musée du Louvre, Paris. Photo Marcel Guiot, Paris.

In the painting, dated 1892, in the collection of Governor and Mrs. Averell Harriman, New York (reproduced in Rewald: *Post-Impressionism*, p. 513), the attitude of the standing nude is somewhat changed; it corresponds to the drawing reproduced on plate 55.

41 TAHITIANS WATCHING A GROUP OF DANCERS, 1891–93

Pencil. Present whereabouts unknown. Photo Marcel Guiot, Paris.

Some elements of this drawing appear in the painting *The Devil Speaks*, reproduced in the catalogue of the Gauguin exhibition, Wildenstein Galleries, New York, April–May, 1946, p. 33, No. 20.

42 STUDY SHEETS WITH ORNAMENTS AND TAHITIAN SCULPTURE, 1891–93(?)

Pencil, 7⅞" x 11¾" (together). Collection Victor Segalen, Paris.

43 STUDY SHEETS WITH ORNA-
MENTS, 1891–93(?)

Pencil and ink, 7⅞″ x 11¾″ (together).
Collection Victor Segalen, Paris.

Numerous studies of ornaments related
to plates 42 and 43 appear as illustrations
in Gauguin's manuscripts *Ancien Culte
Mahorie* (facsimile edition with text by
R. Huyghe, Paris, 1951) and *Noa Noa*
(facsimile edition, Berlin, n.d. [1926]).
See also plate 61.

44 SELF PORTRAITS, 1889–93

Pen and ink. Collection of the late W.
Walter, Paris. Photo Marcel Guiot, Paris.

Although this drawing was part of the
portfolio described in the notice for plate
29, it may have been executed in Brittany, since the lower one of the two
sketches seems related to the painting
Christ in the Garden of Olives, dated
1889, in the Norton Gallery and School
of Art, West Palm Beach, Florida (reproduced in Rewald: *Gauguin*, p. 82).
However, it may also have been done
much later.

45 SELF PORTRAIT, 1891–93

Pencil, 6⅜″ x 4″. Collection Walter R.
Chrysler, Jr., New York. Photo Knoedler & Co., New York.

Page of the sketchbook described in the
notice for plate 34.

46 STUDY SHEET WITH CROUCH-
ING TAHITIAN GIRL, 1891–92

Charcoal. Present whereabouts unknown.
Photo Vizzavona, Paris.

The central figure is a study for the
painting *When Will You Marry? (Nafea*

foa ipoipo), dated 1892, in the Oeffentliche Kunstsammlung, Basel (reproduced
in Rewald: *Gauguin*, p. 116). See also
plate 47.

47 CROUCHING TAHITIAN GIRL,
1891–92

Pencil, charcoal, and pastel, 21¾″ x 18⅞″.
The Art Institute of Chicago (Gift of
Tiffany and Margaret Blake). Photo Wil-
denstein & Co., New York.

See the notice for plate 46. On the other
side of this drawing is the study reproduced on plate 74.

48 VIRGIN MARY AND CHILD
CHRIST (IA ORANA MARIA),
1891(?)

Monotype. Present whereabouts unknown. Photo Vizzavona, Paris.

See also plates 50 and 51, and the notice
for plate 51.

49 TAHITIAN WOMAN WITH TWO
CHILDREN, 1891–93(?)

Monotype. Present whereabouts unknown. Photo Vizzavona, Paris.

The child in the woman's lap has a halo.
The two oxen in the background appear
also, in reverse, in a woodcut ascribed
to Gauguin's second sojourn in the South
Seas, although a proof of it was pasted
by the artist on p. 182 of his manuscript
Noa Noa (Guérin, *op. cit.*, No. 68).

50 IA ORANA MARIA, 1891(?)

Monotype. Estate of W. G. R. Allen,
Boston, Massachusetts. Photo Museum
of Fine Arts, Boston.

See also plates 48 and 51, as well as
Guérin, *op. cit.*, No. 51.

51 IA ORANA MARIA, 1891

Charcoal, 23½″ x 14¾″. Collection Miss L. Lasker, New York.

This is a study for—or more likely a drawing after—Gauguin's famous painting of the same title in the Metropolitan Museum, New York (reproduced in Rewald: *Post-Impressionism*, p. 506). This drawing is dedicated to Count [Antoine] de La Rochefoucauld, editor of the periodical *Le Coeur*, who had purchased the artist's canvas *The Loss of Virginity* (see plate 27). The drawing closely reproduces the main figures of the painting, with considerable variations in fore- and background. Plates 48 and 50, being prints, show the Virgin and Child in reverse.

52 TAHITIAN DRINKING FROM A WATERFALL, 1891–93

Monotype, 11″ x 6¼″. Collection Denis Rouart, Paris.

This monotype was purchased by Henri Rouart from the artist in 1893, after Gauguin's return from Tahiti. There is a painting of the same subject in the São Paulo Museum of Art, also a wood relief (reproduced in J. de Rotonchamp: *Paul Gauguin*, Paris, 1925, opposite p. 194), as well as a watercolor (see plate 53).

53 TAHITIAN DRINKING FROM A WATERFALL, 1891–93

Watercolor, 12½″ x 8½″. The Art Institute of Chicago (Gift of Mrs. Emily Crane Chadbourne).

See also plate 52 and the notice for that plate.

54 JOYOUSNESS (AREAREA), c. 1892(?)

Watercolor in form of fan, 22″ in diameter. Collection Mr. and Mrs. Sidney F. Brody, Los Angeles, California. Photo Wildenstein & Co., New York.

A painting of the same subject is reproduced in Rewald: *Gauguin*, p. 106. It does not seem improbable that this fan was designed *after* the painting, possibly during Gauguin's sojourn in France, 1893–95, when he continued to "exploit" his Tahitian compositions among which this was a particularly noteworthy one.

55 EVE, 1891–92

Pastel, 30⅜″ x 14″. Oeffentliche Kunstsammlung, Basel. Photo Vizzavona, Paris.

Study for the painting *Words of the Devil (Parau 'na te Varua ino)*, dated 1892, in the collection of Governor and Mrs. Averell Harriman, New York. See also plate 40 as well as plate 106. A similar drawing was pasted by the artist into his manuscript *Noa Noa*, Musée du Louvre, Paris, p. 51. The figures of the nude and the devil appear again in a woodcut executed during the artist's second sojourn in the South Seas (see Guérin, *op. cit.*, No. 57). A pen-and-ink sketch of the same subject is in the Art Institute of Chicago.

56 STANDING TAHITIAN NUDE, 1892

Charcoal, 36¼″ x 21⅝″. Private collection, Paris.

Gauguin had already used a similar figure of Eve in a painting executed in 1890 before his departure for Tahiti (see H. Dorra: "The First Eves in Gauguin's Eden," *Gazette des Beaux-Arts*, March,

1953). He was to represent the same figure repeatedly (see plates 57–60; also p. 69 of the manuscript *Noa Noa* and Guérin, *op. cit.*, Nos. 27–29). A. Alexandre: *Paul Gauguin*, Paris, 1930, p. 125, reproduces another painting, *Delicious Earth (Te nave nave fenua)*, in the Museum of Modern Western Art, Moscow, in which this figure also appears.

57 STANDING TAHITIAN NUDE,
c. 1892

Watercolor. Estate of W. G. R. Allen, Boston, Massachusetts. Photo Museum of Fine Arts, Boston.

See notice for plate 56.

58 STANDING TAHITIAN NUDE,
c. 1892

Watercolor. Musée de Grenoble, France. Photo Vizzavona, Paris.

See notice for plate 56.

59 STANDING TAHITIAN NUDE,
c. 1892

Watercolor. National Gallery of Art, Washington, D.C. (Lessing Rosenwald Collection).

This is either a study for—or more probably after—Gauguin's woodcut *Delicious Earth (Te nave nave fenua)*, Guérin, *op. cit.*, Nos. 27–29. The artist's preparatory studies for woodcuts or monotypes are usually reversed in his prints, which is not the case here. The inscription in "pidgin-French," *Pas écouter li li menteur*, is the same one Gauguin used for an earlier and quite different representation of Eve. See notice for plate 22.

60 STANDING TAHITIAN NUDE,
c. 1892

Charcoal, 17¼" x 11¼". Present whereabouts unknown.

See notice for plate 56.

61 TAHITIAN WOMEN, 1891–93(?)

Pencil and pen and ink on parchment, 9¼" x 12⁷⁄₁₆". The Art Institute of Chicago (David Adler Collection).

The two figures seem related to various drawings from the portfolio described in the notice for plate 29. The sleeping woman shows great similarities with No. 26 of that portfolio (reproduced on p. 23 of the catalogue of the Galerie Marcel Guiot exhibition). The ornamental design in the upper right appears connected with similar studies: see plates 42 and 43 and the notice for plate 43.

62 TAHITIAN WOMAN WITH PIG,
c. 1893

Pencil and watercolor, 2⅜" x 6⅝". Collection Mr. and Mrs. Richard Rodgers, New York. Photo Knoedler & Co., New York.

The crouching figure is identical with that of the Tahitian woman in the painting *Alone (Otahi)*, dated 1893, in the Musée du Louvre, Paris.

63 STUDIES OF TAHITIAN WOMEN,
1891–93

Pen and ink and watercolor, 7⅝" x 10⅛". Musée du Louvre, Paris.

This is one of the many drawings, watercolors, and prints that Gauguin pasted into the manuscript *Noa Noa*, which he apparently prepared in France after his return from his first trip to Tahiti. This is p. 185 of the manuscript (see also the facsimile edition), donated to the Louvre by Gauguin's friend G. Daniel de Monfreid. The squatting figure at the right appears also, in a slightly different attitude, in the painting *The Idol* (reproduced in Rewald: *Gauguin*, p. 140), in the background of the painting *Nave nave moe*, in the Museum of Modern Western Art, Moscow (reproduced in E. Wiese: *Paul Gauguin*, Leipzig, 1923, p. 34), and—in reverse—in the painting *Et l'or de leurs corps*, dated 1901, in the Musée du Louvre (reproduced in Rewald, *op. cit.*, p. 145). See also Guérin, *op. cit.*, No. 35. Compare with plate 39.

64 THE SACRED MOUNTAIN (THE SITE OF THE TEMPLE) PARARI TE MARAE, c. 1892

Watercolor. Collection Mrs. Charles Phinney, Cambridge, Massachusetts. Photo Carstairs Gallery, New York.

A painting of the same subject, dated 1892, is in the collection of Mr. and Mrs. R. Meyer de Schauensee, Philadelphia, Pennsylvania (reproduced in the catalogue of the Gauguin exhibition, Wildenstein Galleries, New York, April–May, 1956, p. 50, No. 34).

65 TAHITIAN LANDSCAPE, 1891–93

Watercolor, 10⅜″ x 13¾″. Collection Stavros S. Niarchos, New York. Photo Knoedler & Co., New York.

A practically identical watercolor was pasted by Gauguin on p. 179 of his manuscript *Noa Noa*, now in the Louvre.

66 TAHITIAN HUT UNDER PALM-TREES, 1891–93

Watercolor, 11¾″ x 8¾″. Musée du Louvre, Paris.

This watercolor was pasted by Gauguin on p. 181 of his manuscript *Noa Noa*. See notice for plate 63.

67 PAGE OF A LETTER, 1892

Present whereabouts unknown.

The watercolor sketch is a summary reproduction of Gauguin's painting *The Spirit of the Dead Watches (Manao Tupapao)*, dated 1892, in the collection of A. Conger Goodyear, New York (reproduced in Rewald: *Post-Impressionism*, p. 526). This canvas is one of Gauguin's most important works of his first trip to Tahiti. The accompanying text of the letter gives a short analysis of the meaning of the composition and the colors, repeating explanations also given in letters to G. Daniel de Monfreid and to the artist's wife.

68 PETITES BABIOLES TAHITIENNES (LITTLE TAHITIAN KNICK-KNACKS), 1892

Pencil, charcoal, ink, and watercolor, 17½″ x 12⅝″. Present whereabouts unknown. Photo Knoedler & Co., New York.

The seated figure at the right, seen from the back (which is also sketched in pencil on the reverse of the drawing) appears again in a painting, *Tahitian Women on the Beach*, in the collection of Robert Lehman, New York (reproduced in Rewald: *Post-Impressionism*, p. 508). For nude studies of a woman in the same attitude, see plates 111 and 112.

69 STUDIES OF COWS AND HEAD OF
A DEAD TAHITIAN, 1891–93

Watercolors. Present whereabouts unknown. Photo Marcel Guiot, Paris.

The head of the dead man also appears
in the painting *Royal End* (*Arii mata-
moé*), dated 1892, of which Gauguin
pasted a photograph on p. 59 of his manuscript *Noa Noa*. These study sheets, as
well as those reproduced on plates 70–72,
were part of the portfolio described in
the notice for plate 29.

70 STUDY SHEETS WITH ANIMALS
AND NATIVES, 1891–93

Pencil and watercolor. Present whereabouts unknown. Photo Marcel Guiot,
Paris.

These studies were part of the portfolio
described in the notice for plate 29.

71 DOG, 1891

Watercolor, 3½" x 4⅜". Collection Mr.
and Mrs. Ward Cheney, New York.
Photo Wildenstein & Co., New York.

Study for the painting *Under the Pan-
danus* (*I raro te oviri*), dated 1891, in
the Minneapolis Institute of Arts (reproduced in Rewald: *Post-Impressionism*,
p. 511). This watercolor was part of the
portfolio described in the notice for
plate 29.

72 STUDIES OF A GREYHOUND,
c. 1892

Charcoal and wash, 7" x 10⅞". Wildenstein & Co., New York.

A dog of the same type appears in two
paintings executed in 1892, reproduced
in Rewald: *Gauguin*, pp. 106 and 107.

This study was part of the portfolio described in the notice for plate 29.

73 STUDY SHEET WITH HORSES
AND DOG, 1891–93(?)

Pencil. Collection Victor Segalen, Paris.

74 TAHITIAN GIRL, 1891–93

Charcoal, 21¾" x 18⅞". The Art Institute of Chicago (Gift of Tiffany and
Margaret Blake).

This is the reverse side of the drawing
reproduced on plate 47.

75 HEAD OF A TAHITIAN GIRL
WITH FLOWERS IN HER HAIR,
1891–93(?)

Pencil and blue crayon, 4" x 3⅜". Collection Marcel Guiot, Paris.

Although this drawing was part of the
portfolio described in the notice for plate
29, this head appears only in works which
date from Gauguin's second sojourn in
the South Seas, during which he used it
repeatedly—sometimes with slight variations—in different paintings, such as *Con-
versation* (reproduced in Rewald: *Gauguin*, p. 144), *Maternity*, in the Ittleson
collection, New York (reproduced *ibid.*,
p. 141), and, in reverse, *Contes Barbares*,
dated 1902, in the Folkwang Museum,
Essen, Germany (reproduced *ibid.*, p.
139). It appears also in reverse on p. 129
of Gauguin's manuscript *Avant et Après*
as well as in a woodcut (see Guérin,
op. cit., No. 81).

76 HEAD OF A TAHITIAN WOMAN,
1891

Watercolor, 12⅛" x 9⅜". Collection
Mrs. Diego Suarez, New York. Photo
Wildenstein & Co., New York.

The same figure appears in the painting *Words, Words (Les parao parao)*, dated 1891, in the Museum of Modern Western Art, Moscow (reproduced in Wiese, *op. cit.*, p. 23).

77 THE SAVAGE (OVIRI), 1891–93

Watercolor. Present whereabouts unknown. Photo Vizzavona, Paris.

This watercolor represents a terra-cotta statue by Gauguin, formerly in the collection of G. Daniel de Monfreid. The artist also made a woodcut of this subject (see Guérin, *op. cit.*, No. 48).

78 HERE WE LOVE (TE FARURU), 1891–93

Charcoal, brush, pen and ink. Present whereabouts unknown. Photo Vizzavona, Paris.

Gauguin also made a woodcut of the same subject (see Guérin, *op. cit.*, Nos. 21 and 22).

79 EMBRACE, 1892–93

Watercolor.

An illustrated page from Gauguin's manuscript *Ancien Culte Mahorie*, p. 79. The artist repeated this watercolor on p. 75 of his manuscript *Noa Noa*. On *Ancien Culte Mahorie*, see the facsimile edition, Paris, 1951, with comments by R. Huyghe.

80 TAHITIAN LEGEND, 1892–93

Watercolor.

An illustrated page from Gauguin's manuscript *Ancien Culte Mahorie*, p. 24.

The artist copied the legends assembled in this manuscript from a book by J. A. Moerenhout: *Voyages aux îles du Grand Océan, contenant des documents nouveaux sur la géographie physique et politique, la langue, la littérature, la religion, les moeurs, les usages et les coutumes de leurs habitants*, etc. . . ., 2 volumes, Paris, 1837. See also the notice for plate 79.

81 TAHITIAN LEGEND, 1892–93

Watercolor, 6″ x 9½″. Collection Robert Lehman, New York.

A similar watercolor appears on p. 17 of Gauguin's manuscript *Ancien Culte Mahorie* and on p. 57 of his manuscript *Noa Noa*. See notices for plates 79 and 80.

82 SEATED TAHITIAN BOY, 1891–93

Charcoal. Present whereabouts unknown. Photo Vizzavona, Paris.

There exists a similar drawing which bears the date 1892.

83 MUSIQUE BARBARE, 1891–93

Watercolor on silk, 4¾″ x 8¼″. Private collection, Basel. Photo Vizzavona, Paris.

The mysterious forms to the right of the central head appear also in watercolor illustrations on p. 21 of the manuscript *Ancien Culte Mahorie* and on p. 56 of the *Noa Noa* manuscript.

84 TAHITIAN GIRL, 1891–93

Watercolor, 5½″ x 5¼″. Collection Robert Lehman, New York.

34

A very similar watercolor is to be found on p. 63 of the manuscript *Noa Noa*. The profile sketch at the left may well be a caricature of the artist by himself (see his *Self Portrait*, plate 45).

85 WORDS OF MOON AND EARTH (PARAU HINA TEFATOU), 1891–93

Watercolor. Present whereabouts unknown. Photo Vizzavona, Paris.

The same group appears also as a detail of a woodcut (Guérin, *op. cit.*, No. 31) which Gauguin pasted on p. 57 of his manuscript *Noa Noa*. For a drawing of this group, see Guérin, p. xvii.

86 TWO TAHITIAN WOMEN, 1894(?)

Watercolor, 10¼″ x 7⅞″. Knoedler & Co., New York.

This composition of two women against a decorative background seems to illustrate Odilon Redon's influence on Gauguin.

FRANCE (1893–95)

87 TAHITIAN WOMAN AND IDOL, 1894(?)

Watercolor and pen and ink. Present whereabouts unknown. Photo Vizzavona, Paris.

The same figure, in reverse, appears in the painting *Arearea no varuo ino*, in the Ny Carlsberg Glyptotek, Copenhagen (reproduced in Malingue, *op. cit.*, p. 198). This painting was given by the artist to Mme Gloanec, his hostess at Pont-Aven; the dedication bears the date 1894. This does not necessarily mean that the canvas was painted at Pont-Aven, for Gauguin could have brought it with him when he went there, unlikely though this seems. Since he made many woodcuts at Pont-Aven, all concerned with Tahitian subjects, it appears very possible that the painting was also executed in Brittany. Moreover, the composition of the canvas, with its pronounced diagonals and the two small figures in the background, is strangely reminiscent of Gauguin's canvas *Jacob Wrestling with the Angel*, one of the most important works of his earlier Breton period (reproduced in Rewald: *Post-Impressionism*, p. 203). But this does not prove that the present watercolor was also made in Brittany. (*Arearea* means "joyousness"; *no varua ino* concerns the devil.)

88 HEAD OF A BRETON WOMAN, 1888–90 or 1894

Gouache. Present whereabouts unknown. Photo Vizzavona, Paris.

Since this head does not seem connected with any of Gauguin's known paintings from Brittany, it appears impossible to date it with precision. It would seem, however, that it may have been done after his return from his first trip to Tahiti.

89 TWO BRETON WOMEN HARVESTING, 1888–90 or 1894

Charcoal, 11⅞″ x 7⅞″. Collection Richard Lee Feigen, Los Angeles, California.

This broadly conceived sketch seems connected with Gauguin's search for a "Synthetist" style of the years 1888–90 (there are a few similar studies in a sketchbook dating from that period; see R. Huyghe: *Le Carnet de Gauguin*, Paris, 1952). On the back of this sheet, however, is a watercolor sketch that resembles more closely some of his Tahitian studies (see plate 91).

90 STILL LIFE (*Brittany*), 1888–90 or 1894

Gouache, 15¾″ x 24¼″. Wildenstein & Co., New York.

The presence of the lower part of a seated Idol in the upper left corner seems to indicate that this still life—one of Gauguin's largest gouaches—may have been painted after his return from Tahiti. It is conceivable, though, that it dates from his long sojourn in Brittany, 1888–90, during which he submitted to the influence of Cézanne and elaborated his "Synthetist" style of which this work is a striking example.

91 STUDIES OF BRETON CHILDREN, 1888–90 or 1894

Charcoal and watercolor, 11⅞″ x 7⅞″. Collection Richard Lee Feigen, Los Angeles, California.

This is the verso of the drawing reproduced on plate 89. The two figures appear closely related to similar studies which Gauguin made in Tahiti (see plate 36).

TAHITI AND DOMINIQUE
(1895–1903)

92 HEAD OF A TAHITIAN MAN, 1895–1903(?)

Black and red crayon, 12¾″ x 11″. The Art Institute of Chicago (Gift of Emily Crane Chadbourne).

93 HEAD OF A TAHITIAN WOMAN, 1891(?)

Pencil, 12¹¹⁄₁₆″ x 9⅝″. The Cleveland Museum of Art (Mr. and Mrs. Lewis B. Williams Collection).

A very similar head appears in the painting *Words, Words*, dated 1891, in the Museum of Modern Western Art, Moscow (reproduced in Wiese, *op. cit.*, p. 23). See the notice for plate 76.

94 HEAD OF A TAHITIAN WOMAN, 1895–1903(?)

Watercolor, 12¼″ x 7⅜″. Knoedler & Co., New York. Photo César M. de Hauke, Paris.

95 HEAD OF A TAHITIAN WOMAN, 1895–1903(?)

Charcoal. Knoedler & Co., New York. Photo Curt Valentin Gallery.

96 ROCKY COAST (*Tahiti?*), 1895–1903(?)

Charcoal. Collection Victor Segalen, Paris.

97 TAHITIAN LANDSCAPE, 1895–1903(?)

Monotype. Collection Lessing Rosenwald, Jenkintown, Pennsylvania.

98 LETTER TO AN UNKNOWN COLLECTOR, 1896

Pen and ink, 10″ x 7½″. Collection Mr. and Mrs. Alex M. Lewyt, New York. Photo Wildenstein & Co., New York.

This letter originally accompanied a small painting on a wooden panel, dated 1896; it tells the future owner of the work how to frame and preserve it. The sketch represents the main figures of a woodcut *The Food of the Gods* (*Ma-*

hana atua), which Gauguin had executed during his first sojourn in Tahiti. See Guérin, *op. cit.*, Nos. 42 and 43.

99 DECORATIVE PERSON, 1903

Pen and ink, 11⅝" x 8½".

Illustration (p. 121) of Gauguin's manuscript *Avant et Après*, dated 1903. This drawing repeats in reverse the figure of the lying nude represented in plate 100. See also the woodcuts of the same subject, Guérin, *op. cit.*, Nos. 62 and 80.

100 WOMAN WITH MANGOS (TE ARII VAHINE), 1896

Watercolor, 7½" x 9½". Collection Mr. and Mrs. Ward Cheney, New York. Photo Fine Arts Associates, New York. This watercolor is a study for—or more likely after—a painting of the same title, dated 1896, in the Museum of Modern Western Art, Moscow (reproduced in Rewald: *Gauguin*, p. 118).

101 STUDY FOR "WHENCE DO WE COME? WHAT ARE WE? WHERE ARE WE GOING?" 1898

Charcoal. Present whereabouts unknown. Photo Vizzavona, Paris.

The squares on the drawing indicate that it was the "working study" which Gauguin used to transpose the composition on the large canvas (55½" x 148¼"). This canvas, in the Museum of Fine Arts, Boston, is the artist's largest and doubtless also most important work. He painted it early in 1898 when—unable to stand any longer the life of intermittent illness and increasing debts he was leading in Tahiti—he resolved to kill himself. But before doing so, he de-

cided to draw upon all his remaining strength to execute a last composition, as it were, his last testament. His suicide attempt having failed, he later returned to his hut for more sufferings, more disillusions, and more work.

102 TAHITIAN NATIVES, PEACOCK, AND ANGEL, c. 1902

Monotype, 5⅞" x 9½". The Art Institute of Chicago (Gift of Emily Crane Chadbourne).

There exists a painting of the same subject, dated 1902, reproduced in Rewald: *Gauguin*, p. 143. The angel and the group of three natives also appear in two separate drawings in the manuscript *Avant et Après*, pp. 123 and 119 respectively.

103 COVER FOR THE MANUSCRIPT "L'ESPRIT MODERNE ET LE CATHOLICISME," 1897–98

Monotype and pen and ink, 12½" x 7½". The City Art Museum of St. Louis (Gift of Vincent Price).

On this important document, see H. Stewart Leonard: "An Unpublished Manuscript by Paul Gauguin," *Bulletin of the City Art Museum of St. Louis*, summer, 1949. See also plate 104.

104 TAHITIAN NATIVITY, 1897–98

Monotype. The City Art Museum of St. Louis (Gift of Vincent Price).

Illustration of the manuscript described in the notice for plate 103. A related drawing appears on p. 205 of the manuscript *Avant et Après*. Similar figures can be found also in a painting of the *Nativity*, dated 1902, reproduced on

p. 64 of the catalogue of the Gauguin exhibition, Wildenstein Gallery, New York, April–May, 1956, No. 52.

105 STUDY FOR "TE PAPE NAVE NAVE," 1898

Charcoal. Present whereabouts unknown. Photo Vizzavona, Paris.

The painting, dated 1898, for which this is a preparatory drawing, repeats some of the elements of *Whence Do We Come? What Are We? Where Are We Going?* and is scarcely less important. It is in the collection of Mr. and Mrs. Leigh B. Block, Chicago, Illinois, and is reproduced on p. 60 of the catalogue of the Gauguin exhibition, Wildenstein Gallery, New York, April–May, 1956, No. 60.

106 THE NIGHTMARE, 1895–1901(?)

Monotype, 23″ x 17″. Wildenstein & Co., New York.

The figure of the nude girl had already appeared much earlier in Gauguin's work (see plate 55 and the notice for that plate). He represented her again in a woodcut executed during his second sojourn in the South Seas (Guérin, *op. cit.*, No. 57). The devil on horseback in this monotype is shown also in a painting of 1901 (reproduced in Malingue, *op. cit.*, p. 229) as well as in a monotype and a watercolor (see plates 107 and 108).

107 THE ESCAPE, c. 1901

Monotype. Present whereabouts unknown. Photo Vizzavona, Paris.

The figure on horseback shows the features with which Gauguin generally represented the devil. It appears also in the background of *The Nightmare* (plate 106), in a painting dated 1901 (see notice for plate 106), and in a watercolor (see plate 108).

108 THE ESCAPE, c. 1901

Watercolor. Present whereabouts unknown. Photo Vizzavona, Paris.

See also plates 106 and 107, and the notices for these plates.

109 TAHITIAN MAN WITH TWO CHILDREN, c. 1902

Monotype. Present whereabouts unknown. Photo Vizzavona, Paris.

The figure of the man appears also at the extreme right of the painting *The Sister of Charity*, dated 1902, in the Marion Koogler McNay Art Institute, San Antonio, Texas (reproduced in Malingue, *op. cit.*, p. 228). This monotype is apparently a preparatory study for the painting. See also plate 110.

110 TAHITIAN NATIVES WITH CHILD, c. 1902

Monotype. Present whereabouts unknown. Photo Vizzavona, Paris.

The figure of the man as well as that of the woman (sketched only indistinctly and in reverse in the monotype reproduced on plate 109) appear together in the painting *The Sister of Charity*, dated 1902. See notice for plate 109.

111 CROUCHING TAHITIAN WOMAN SEEN FROM THE BACK, c. 1902

Monotype, 19″ x 11½″. Collection Mr. and Mrs. Richard S. Davis, Minneapolis,

Minnesota. Photo Wildenstein & Co., New York.

A similar figure, partly dressed, had already appeared in a painting dating from Gauguin's first sojourn in Tahiti, *Tahitian Women on the Beach*, collection of Robert Lehman, New York (reproduced in Rewald: *Post-Impressionism*, p. 508). See also plate 68. The same figure in the nude, with the head slightly turned to the right, can be found in the painting *The Call*, dated 1902, in the Cleveland Museum of Art (reproduced in Rewald: *Gauguin*, p. 134). See also plate 112.

112 CROUCHING TAHITIAN WOMAN SEEN FROM THE BACK, c. 1902

Monotype in black and ochre, 12⅝″ x 10½″. Private collection, New York. Photo Wildenstein & Co., New York.

See plate 111 and the notice for that plate. The same figure appears in an identical pose in a painting dated 1902 (reproduced in Wiese, *op. cit.*, p. 42).

113 THE CALL, c. 1902

Pencil. Present whereabouts unknown. Photo Jacques Dubourg, Paris.

Study for the two foreground figures of the painting in the Cleveland Museum of Art (reproduced in Rewald: *Gauguin*, p. 134). For other studies related to the same painting, see plates 111, 112, and 114, as well as 115; also pp. 165 and 175 of the facsimile edition of *Avant et Après*.

114 STUDY FOR "THE CALL," c. 1902

Monotype. Museum of Fine Arts, Boston.

This monotype represents the two foreground figures—the one to the left drawn twice—of the painting *The Call*, dated 1902. See also plate 113 and the notice for that plate.

115 HEADS OF TWO TAHITIAN WOMEN, c. 1902

Monotype. Collection César M. de Hauke, Paris.

Study for a painting reproduced in Alexandre, *op. cit.*, p. 189. These heads are, with slight variations, those of the two central figures of the painting *The Call*. See plates 113 and 114, and the notice for plate 113.

116. HEADS OF TWO TAHITIAN WOMEN, c. 1902

Monotype. Collection Lee A. Ault, New York.

117 HEADS OF TWO TAHITIAN WOMEN, c. 1902

Monotype, 18⅛″ x 13½″. Collection Lessing J. Rosenwald, Jenkintown, Pennsylvania.

The same heads appear also in the painting of two Tahitian women in a hut reproduced in Rewald: *Gauguin*, p. 138, except that the upper one faces to the right. This painting is dated 1902. A similar drawing is to be found on p. 155 of the manuscript *Avant et Après*. See also plate 116.

118 TAHITIAN GIRL WITH FLOWER IN HER HAIR, c. 1900(?)

Pastel, 23¾″ x 20¼″. Brooklyn Museum.

119 NOT WITHOUT FEELING, 1903
Pen and ink, 11⅝″ x 8½″.

Illustration (p. 125) of the manuscript
Avant et Après.

120 TAHITIAN WOMAN AND DEVIL,
1900–03(?)

Monotype. Present whereabouts unknown. Photo Vizzavona, Paris.

121 TAHITIAN WOMAN AND DEVIL,
1900–03(?)

Monotype. Present whereabouts unknown. Photo Vizzavona, Paris.

122 HOLY IMAGES, 1903

Pen and ink, 11⅝″ x 8½″.

Illustration (p. 105) of the manuscript
Avant et Après. This drawing attests
to the strange preoccupation with Brittany subjects which appears in the
works of Gauguin's last year, spent at
Atuana on Dominique Island in the
Marquesas. The central group is a reversed reproduction of a moss-covered
stone Pietà from a Breton Calvary
which the artist had represented in the
painting *The Calvary—Green Christ*,
dated 1889, in the Royal Museum of
Fine Arts, Brussels (see Rewald: *Post-
Impressionism*, pp. 304–06). This Breton
Calvary is here surrounded by various
images of Gauguin's South Sea "repertory": peacock, mask of the devil, Tahitian Virgin with Child (see also the
woodcut, Guérin, *op. cit.*, Nos. 60 and
61). Gauguin featured this Calvary in
still another woodcut of the same period
(Guérin, *op. cit.*, No. 68).

123 WHAT ARE YOU THINKING OF?
—I DON'T KNOW, 1903

Pen and ink, 11⅝″ x 8½″.

Illustration (p. 103) of the manuscript
Avant et Après.

124 CHANGE OF RESIDENCE, 1902–03

Monotype.

Illustration of the manuscript *Avant et
Après*. Gauguin represented the same
subject in a painting dated 1902 (reproduced in Rewald: *Gauguin*, p. 142), and
repeated three of the figures in another
canvas, *Woman on a White Horse*,
dated 1903, in the Museum of Fine Arts,
Boston. A similar composition appears
also in a woodcut (see Guérin, *op. cit.*,
No. 66).

125 TAHITIAN COUPLE WALKING,
1900–03(?)

Monotype. Present whereabouts unknown. Photo Vizzavona, Paris.

Gauguin showed the male figure alone
in a woodcut, *Man Carrying Wild
Bananas* (Guérin, *op. cit.*, No. 64), from
the artist's second sojourn in the South
Seas. A monotype of a younger man in
the same attitude appears in the manuscript *Avant et Après* on p. 153.

126 SELF PORTRAIT, 1900–03(?)

Pencil, 5⅞″ x 4″. Collection Victor
Segalen, Paris.

This is apparently one of the artist's last
Self Portraits. It was found in his hut
among his belongings after his death and
auctioned off at Papeete in 1903 with
Gauguin's entire estate. It was acquired
there, together with many other ob-
jects, paintings, drawings, and prints, by
Dr. Segalen, a physician of the French
Navy, friend of G. Daniel de Monfreid.

PLATES

1 HEAD OF A WOMAN   c. 1884

2 STUDIES OF A WOMAN'S HEAD 1884–85

3 PORTRAIT OF THE ARTIST'S SON, CLOVIS
c. 1885

4 PORTRAIT OF PAUL GAUGUIN BY PISSARRO—   c. 1883
PORTRAIT OF CAMILLE PISSARRO BY GAUGUIN

5 PORTRAIT OF CAMILLE PISSARRO   1880

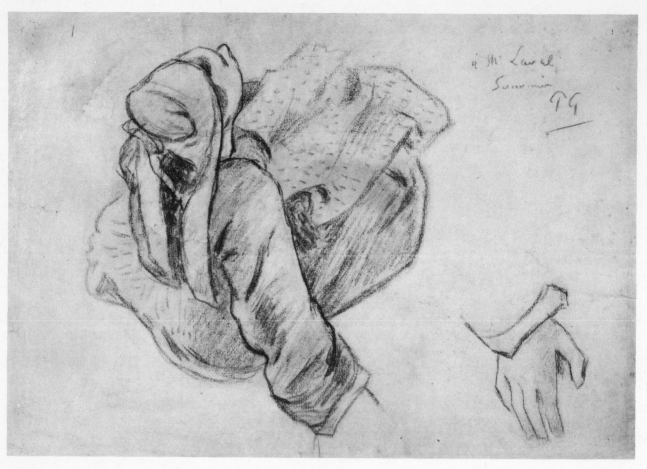

6 SEATED BRITTANY WOMAN   1886(?)

7 TWO WOMEN FROM MARTINIQUE   1887

8 HEAD OF A BRETON WOMAN   1888–90

9 HEAD OF A BRETON BOY   c. 1888

11 YOUNG BRETON GIRL KNITTING 1889

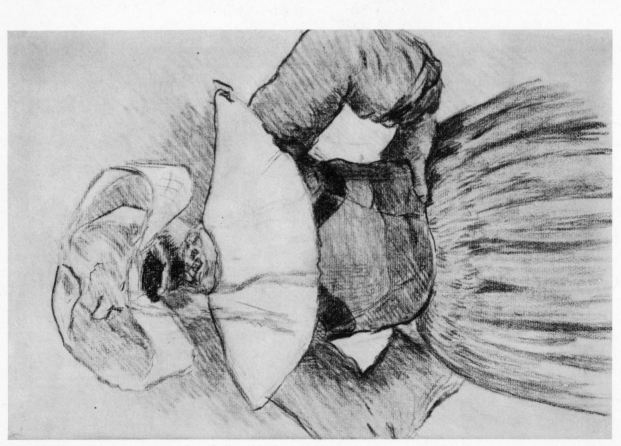

10 BRETON WOMAN SEEN FROM THE BACK c. 1888

1887(?)

13 WOMAN BATHER IN BRITTANY

1888

12. YOUNG BRETON BATHER

14 HEAD OF A BRETON GIRL   c. 1889(?)

15 L'ARLÉSIENNE   1888

16 WASHERWOMEN AT ARLES   1888

17 WASHERWOMEN AT ARLES   1888

18 PEASANT GIRL AT LE POULDU (*Brittany*)   1889

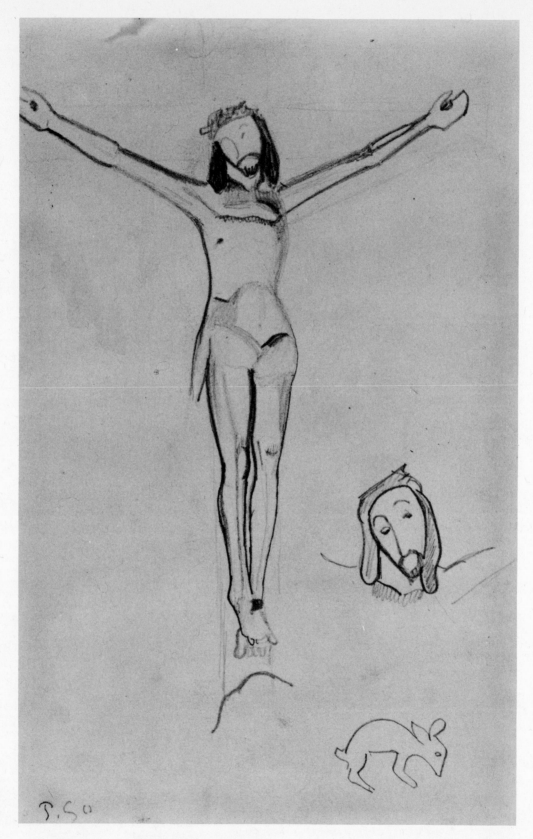

19 STUDY FOR "THE YELLOW CHRIST"   1889

20 THE YELLOW CHRIST   1889

21 MISÈRES HUMAINES (*Brittany*)　　　　　　　　　　　　　　　c. 1888

22 EVE   c. 1889

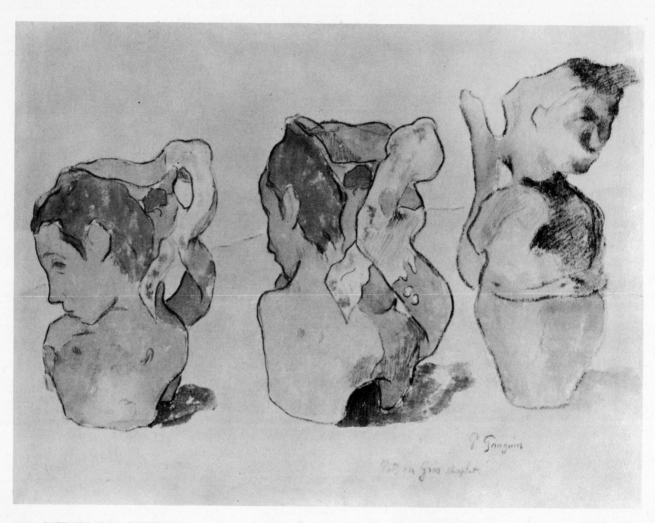

23 STUDIES FOR POTTERY   1887–89

24 LES FOLIES DE L' [AMOUR]   1890

25 NIRVANA—PORTRAIT OF JACOB MEYER DE HAAN (*Brittany*)   c. 1890

26 STUDY FOR A PORTRAIT OF JACOB MEYER DE HAAN (*Brittany*)
c. 1890

27 YOUNG GIRL AND FOX—STUDY FOR "LOSS OF VIRGINITY" (*Paris*)   1890–91

29 HEAD OF A CHILD   c. 1890

28 PORTRAIT OF STÉPHANE MALLARMÉ   1891

30 SOYEZ SYMBOLISTE—PORTRAIT OF JEAN MORÉAS   1890-91

32 HEAD OF A YOUNG TAHITIAN BOY, TETUA   c. 1891

31 HEAD OF A TAHITIAN CHILD   c. 1891

34 HEAD OF A YOUNG TAHITIAN BOY, TASA   C. 1891

33 HEAD OF A YOUNG TAHITIAN BOY, FARE   C. 1891

35 SKETCHES (*Tahiti*)   1891–93

36 SKETCHES (*Tahiti*)   1891–93

37 TAHITIAN GIRL STRETCHED OUT   c. 1893

38 TAHITIAN WOMAN SQUATTING   1891–93(?)

39 CROUCHING TAHITIAN GIRL   1891–93

40 STUDY FOR "WORDS OF THE DEVIL" 1891–92
(PARAU NA TE VARUA INO)

41 TAHITIANS WATCHING A GROUP OF DANCERS   1891–93

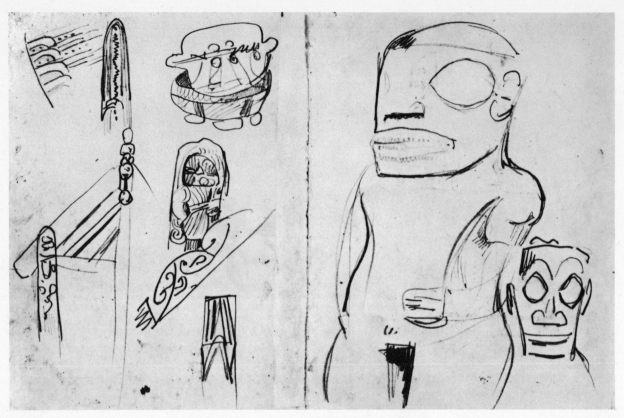

42 STUDY SHEETS WITH ORNAMENTS AND TAHITIAN SCULPTURE   1891–93(?)

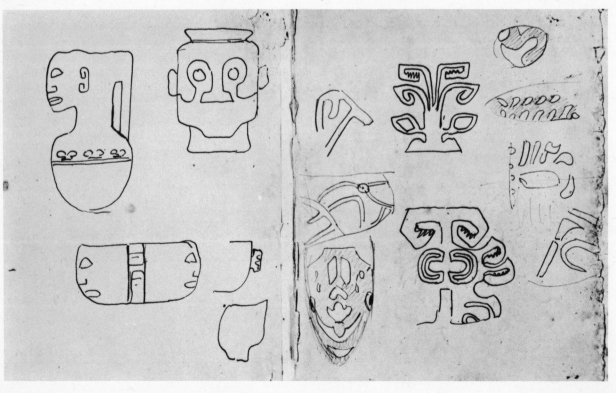

43 STUDY SHEETS WITH ORNAMENTS   1891–93(?)

44 SELF PORTRAITS   1889–93

45 SELF PORTRAIT   1891–93

46 STUDY SHEET WITH CROUCHING TAHITIAN GIRL

47 CROUCHING TAHITIAN GIRL   1891-92

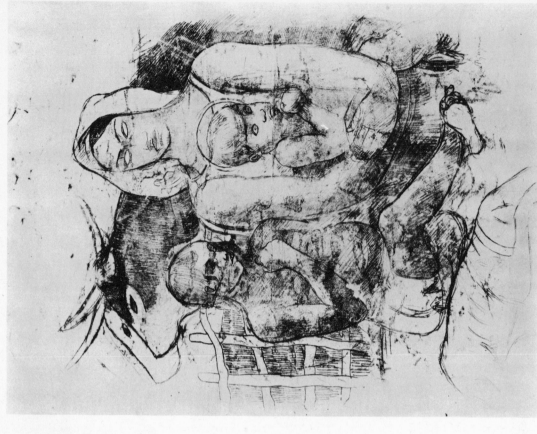

49 TAHITIAN WOMAN WITH TWO CHILDREN   1891–93 (?)

48 VIRGIN MARY AND CHILD CHRIST (IA ORANA MARIA)
1891 (?)

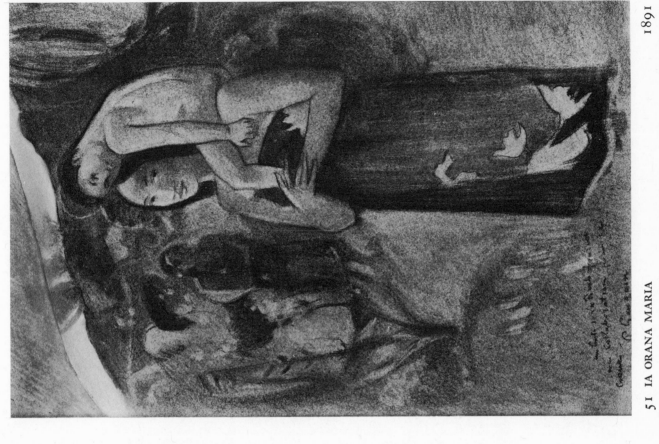

1891

51 IA ORANA MARIA

1891(?)

50 IA ORANA MARIA

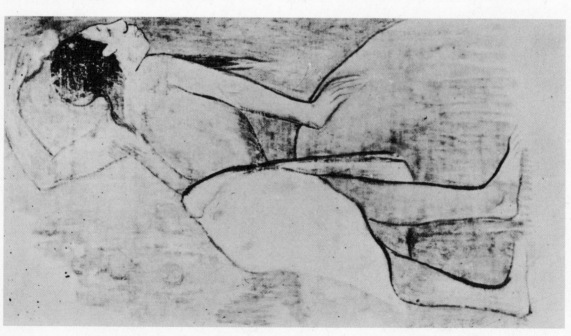

53 TAHITIAN DRINKING FROM A WATERFALL 1891–93

52 TAHITIAN DRINKING FROM A WATERFALL 1891–93

54 JOYOUSNESS (AREAREA)   c. 1892 (?)

55 EVE   1891–92

56 STANDING TAHITIAN NUDE   1892

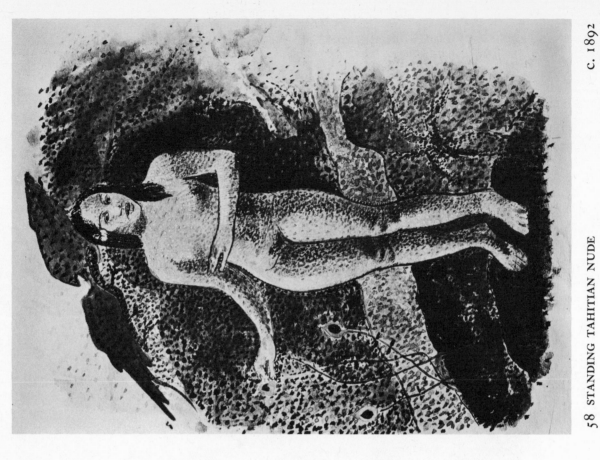

c. 1892

58 STANDING TAHITIAN NUDE

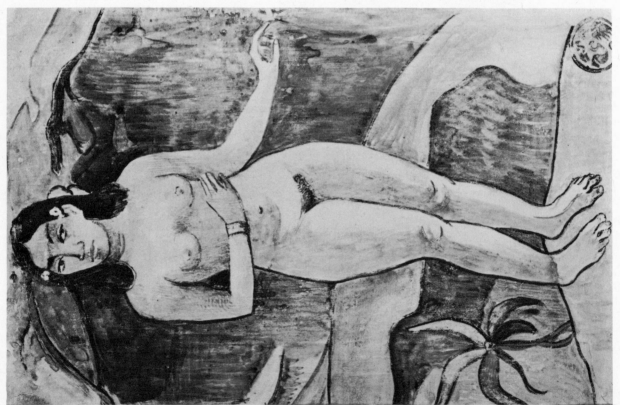

c. 1892

57 STANDING TAHITIAN NUDE

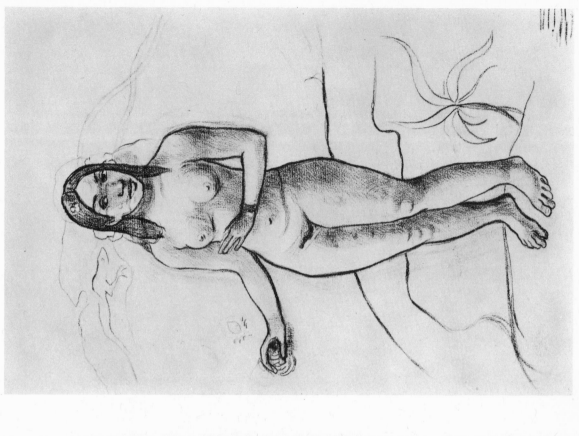

c. 1892

60 STANDING TAHITIAN NUDE

c. 1892

59 STANDING TAHITIAN NUDE

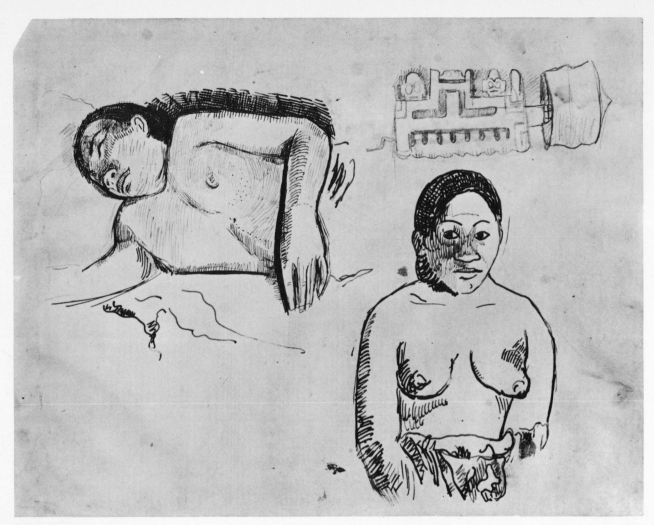

61 TAHITIAN WOMEN   1891–93(?)

62 TAHITIAN WOMAN WITH PIG   c. 1893

63 STUDIES OF TAHITIAN WOMEN   1891–93

64 THE SACRED MOUNTAIN (THE SITE OF THE   c. 1892
TEMPLE—PARARI TE MARAE)

65 TAHITIAN LANDSCAPE   1891–93

66 TAHITIAN HUT UNDER PALMTREES   1891–93

Récapitulons - Partie musicale - Lignes horizontal[es]
ondulantes - accords d'orangé et de bleu[s]
reliés par des jaunes et des violets leurs
dérivés - Éclairés par étincelles verdâtres -
Partie littéraire - L'esprit d'une vivante lié
à l'esprit des Morts - La nuit et le jour.

   Cette genèse est écrite pour ceux qui
veulent toujours savoir les pourquoi les
Parceque -
Sinon c'est tout simplement une étude
de nu océanien.

Petites Babioles Tahitiennes.

à Monsieur de Marolles
Comme un Bon Souvenir de notre entrevue
chez les Maories.

Paul Gauguin
1892.

Taoto

OpuOpu

68 PETITES BABIOLES TAHITIENNES (LITTLE TAHITIAN KNICK-KNACKS)   1892

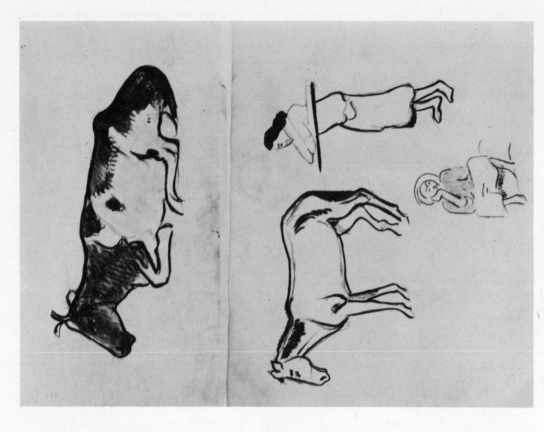

70 STUDY SHEETS WITH ANIMALS AND NATIVES 1891-93

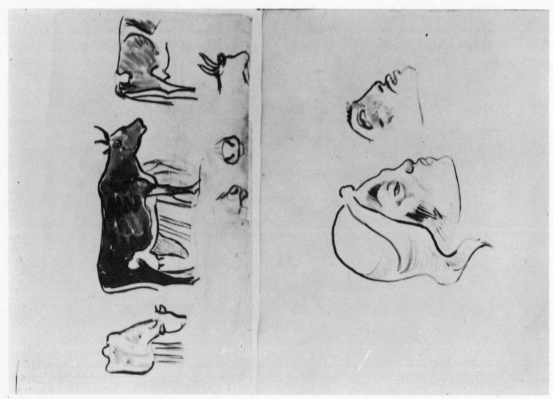

69 STUDIES OF COWS AND HEAD OF A DEAD TAHITIAN
1891-93

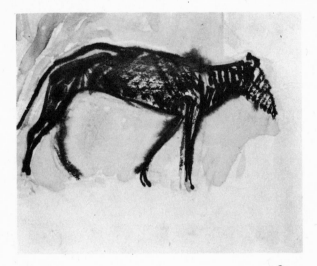

71 DOG   1891

73 STUDY SHEET WITH HORSES AND DOGS
                    1891–93(?)

72 STUDIES OF A GREYHOUND   c. 1892

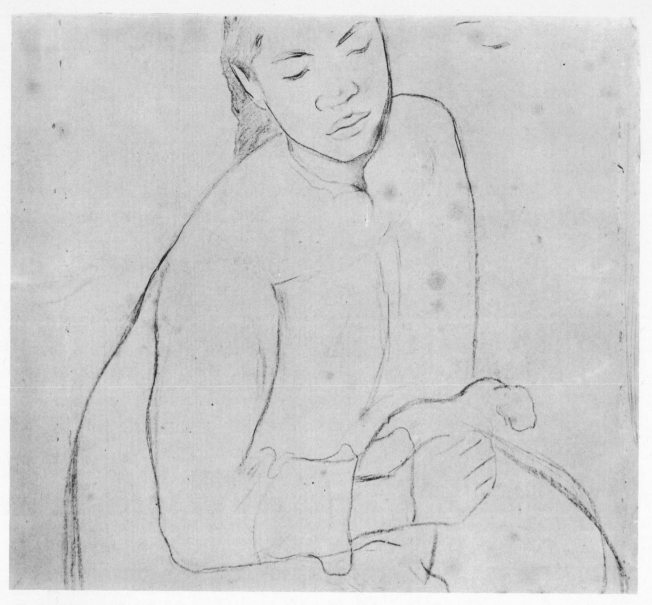

74 TAHITIAN GIRL   1891–93

75 HEAD OF A TAHITIAN GIRL
WITH FLOWERS IN HER HAIR
1891–93(?)

76 HEAD OF A TAHITIAN WOMAN   1891

77 THE SAVAGE (OVIRI)   1891-93

78 HERE WE LOVE (TE FARURU)   1891–93

de leurs trompettes et à battre de leurs
tambours, ce qui était le signal de la
retraite et de la fin de la fête. Le roi
retournait alors à sa demeure, accompagné
de sa suite.

79 EMBRACE   1892–93

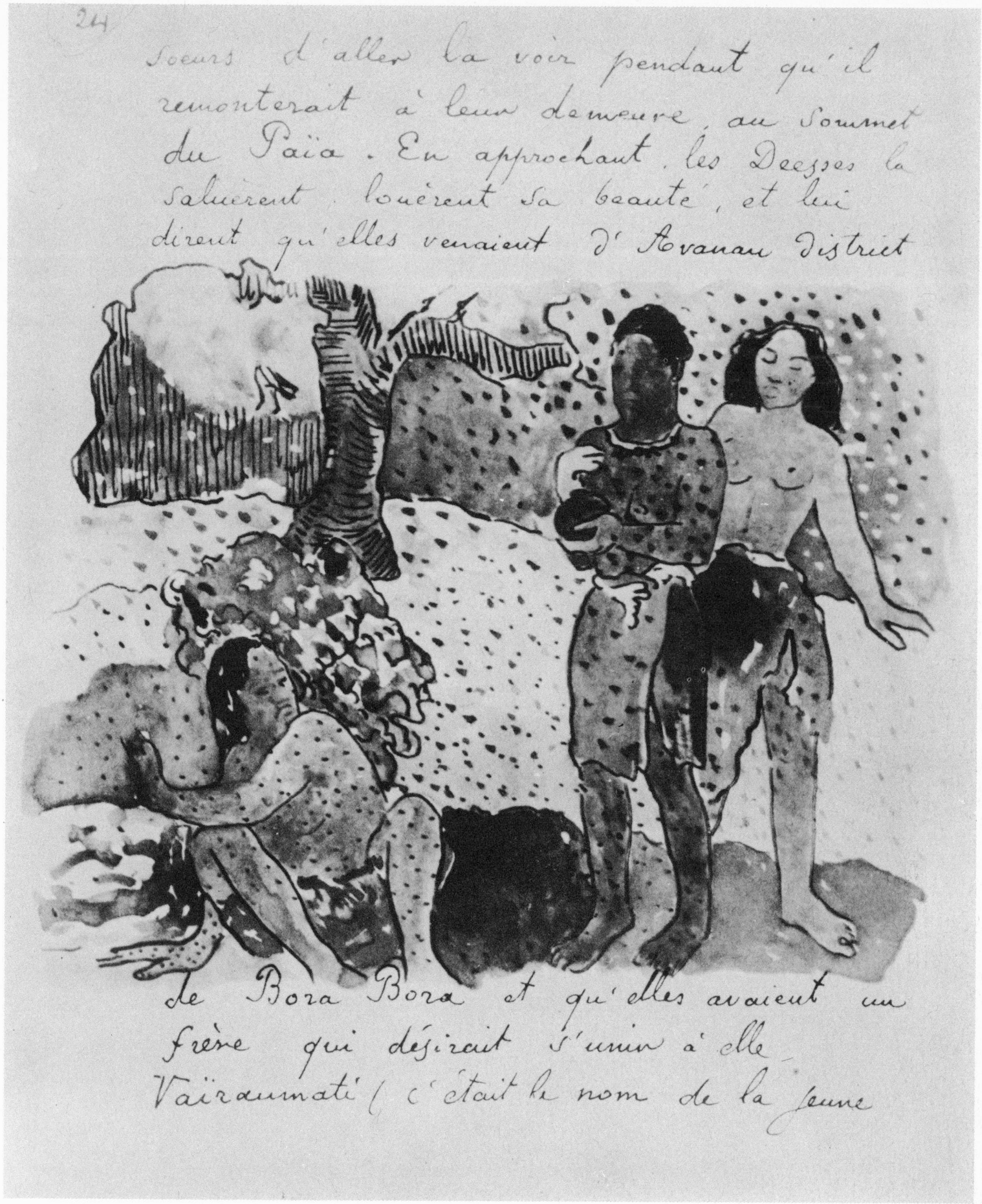
24

soeurs d'aller la voir pendant qu'il
remonterait à leur demeure, au sommet
du Païa. En approchant, les Deesses la
saluèrent, louèrent sa beauté, et lui
dirent qu'elles venaient d'Avanau district

de Bora Bora et qu'elles avaient un
frère qui désirait s'unir à elle.
Vaïraumati (c'était le nom de la jeune

80 TAHITIAN LEGEND 1892–93

81 TAHITIAN LEGEND   1892–93

82 SEATED TAHITIAN BOY   1891–93

83 MUSIQUE BARBARE   1891–93

84 TAHITIAN GIRL   1891–93

85 WORDS OF MOON AND EARTH (PARAU HINA TEFATOU)   1891-93

86 TWO TAHITIAN WOMEN   1894(?)

87 TAHITIAN WOMAN AND IDOL   1894(?)

88 HEAD OF A BRETON WOMAN   1888–90 or 1894

89 TWO BRETON WOMEN HARVESTING   1888–90 or 1894

90 STILL LIFE (*Brittany*)   1888–90 or 1894

91 STUDIES OF BRETON CHILDREN   1888–90 or 1894

92 HEAD OF A TAHITIAN MAN   1895–1903(?)

93 HEAD OF A TAHITIAN WOMAN   1891(?)

94 HEAD OF A TAHITIAN WOMAN   1895–1903(?)

95 HEAD OF A TAHITIAN WOMAN   1895–1903(?)

96 ROCKY COAST (*Tahiti?*)   1895–1903(?)

97 TAHITIAN LANDSCAPE   1895–1903(?)

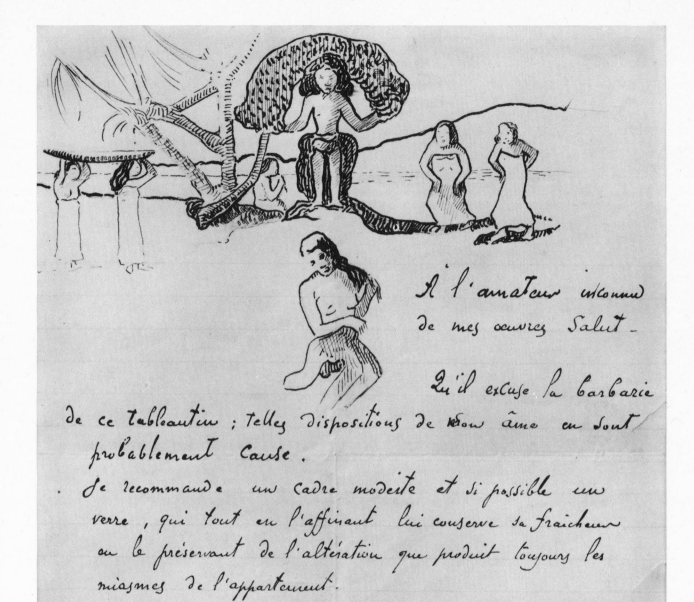

À l'amateur inconnu
de mes œuvres Salut —

Qu'il excuse la barbarie
de ce tableautin ; telles dispositions de mon âme en sont
probablement cause.

. Je recommande un cadre modeste et si possible un
verre, qui tout en l'affinant lui conserve sa fraicheur
en le préservant de l'altération que produit toujours les
miasmes de l'appartement.

Paul Gauguin

Decorative personne _ ..

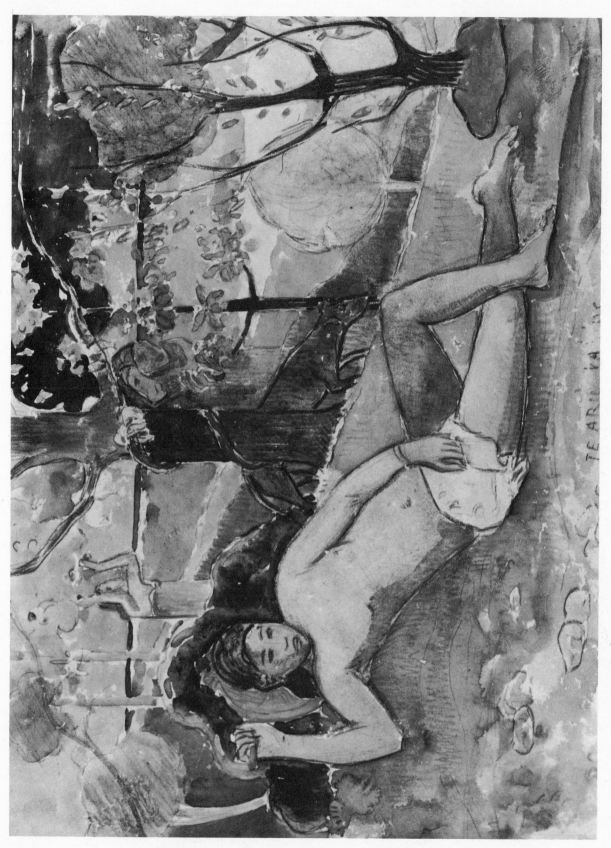

100 WOMAN WITH MANGOS (TE ARII VAHINE) 1896

1898

101 STUDY FOR "WHENCE DO WE COME? WHAT ARE WE?
     WHERE ARE WE GOING?"

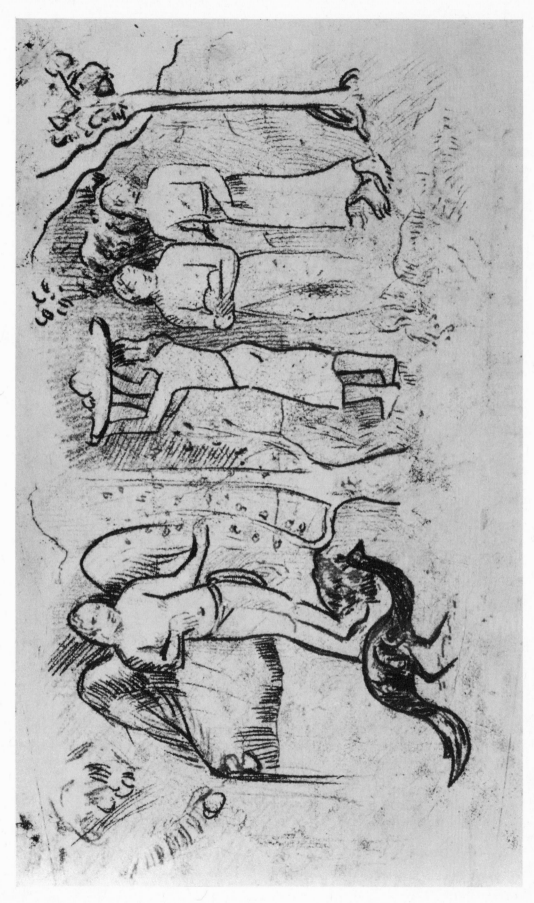

102 TAHITIAN NATIVES, PEACOCK, AND ANGEL

103 BACK COVER FOR THE MANUSCRIPT "L'ESPRIT MODERNE
ET LE CATHOLICISME"   1897–98

104 TAHITIAN NATIVITY   1897-98

105 STUDY FOR "TE PAPE NAVE NAVE"   1898

106 THE NIGHTMARE

1895–1901(?)

107 THE ESCAPE   C. 1901

108 THE ESCAPE   C. 1901

109 TAHITIAN MAN WITH TWO CHILDREN   C. 1902

110 TAHITIAN NATIVES WITH CHILD   C. 1902

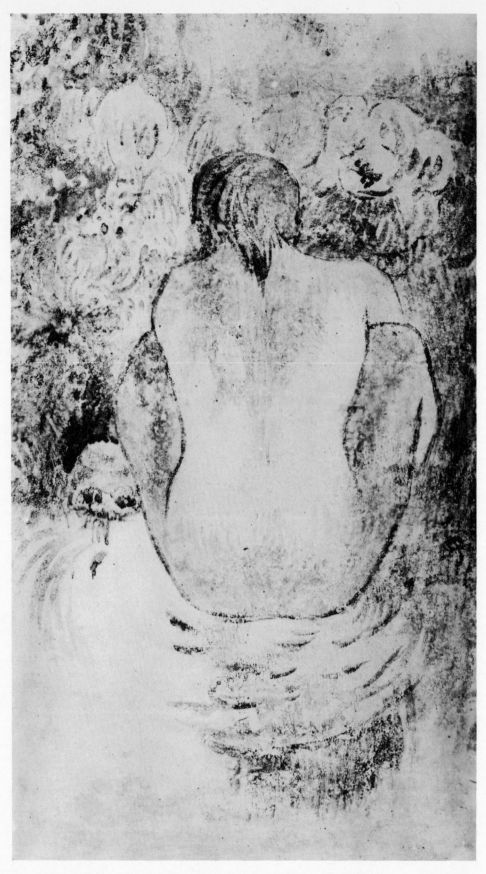

111 CROUCHING TAHITIAN WOMAN SEEN FROM THE BACK   C. 1902

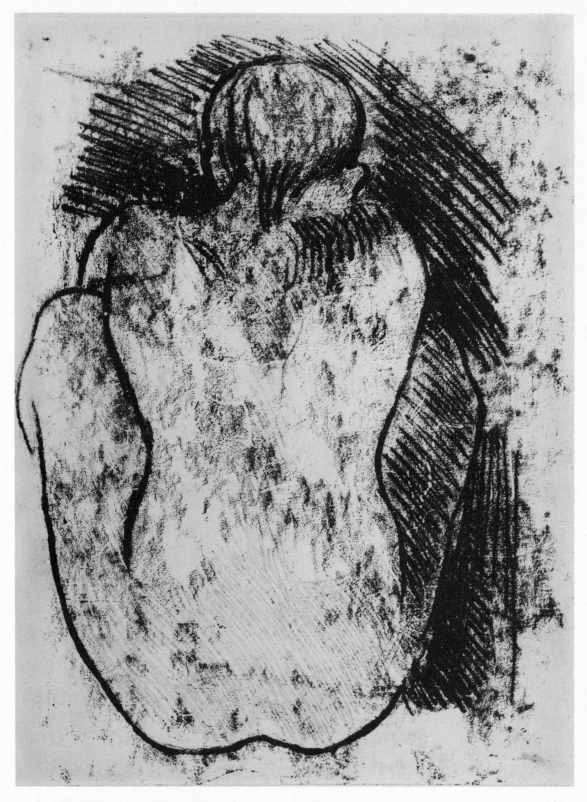

112 CROUCHING TAHITIAN WOMAN SEEN FROM THE BACK   C. 1902

113 THE CALL   C. 1902

114 STUDY FOR "THE CALL"   C. 1902

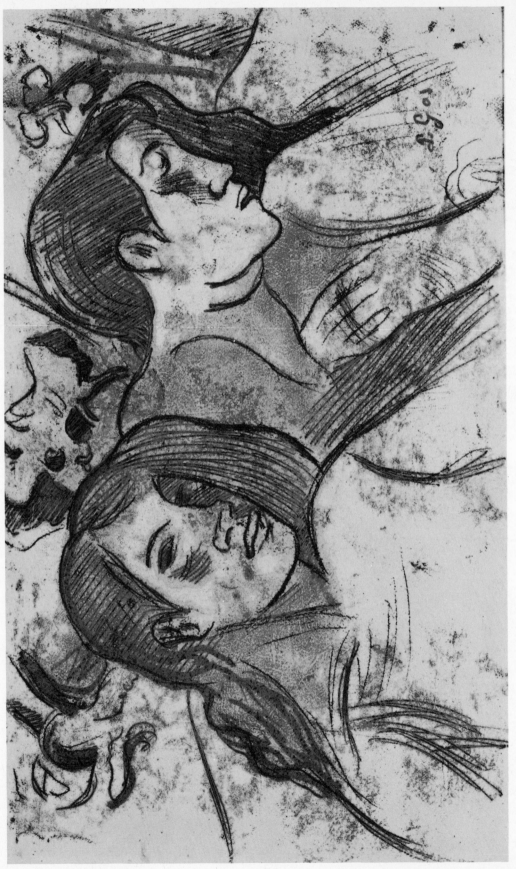

C. 1902

115 HEADS OF TWO TAHITIAN WOMEN

117 HEADS OF TWO TAHITIAN WOMEN

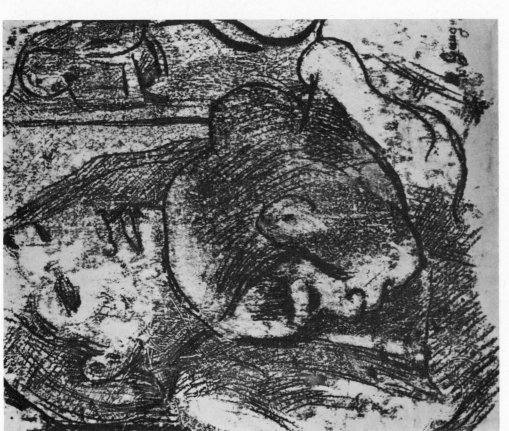

C. 1902

116 HEADS OF TWO TAHITIAN WOMEN

118 TAHITIAN GIRL WITH FLOWER IN HER HAIR   c. 1900(?)

non dépourvues de sentiment. 2G.

1903

120 TAHITIAN WOMAN AND DEVIL   1900–03 (?)

121 TAHITIAN WOMAN AND DEVIL   1900–03 (?)

Les saintes images.

à quoi penses tu ? Je ne sais pas.

123 WHAT ARE YOU THINKING OF?—I DON'T KNOW   1903

Changement de résidence.

P. S.

125 TAHITIAN COUPLE WALKING   1900–03(?)

126 SELF PORTRAIT   1900–03 (?)